Your author, Terry Siciliano, [illegible] a class by herself. How many authors can you name who write and pay to self-publish a book, only to give it away to those in prison?

A couple of years ago, Terry sent us multiple cases of “Beyond a Reasonable Doubt”. Then a few months ago, she contacted me saying she found a few more cases in the attic by the Christmas decorations! She sent those to us as well. They are all gone – all sent to prisons around the country.

In addition to piloting airplanes and writing books, Terry is a volunteer CLI Bible Minister. She reviews the answers from the CLI correspondence Bible study for prison inmates. She truly has a heart for the imprisoned and seeks to give them a hope and purpose through faith in Jesus Christ.

Enjoy her book!

Anders Skaar – Christian Library International – Raleigh NC

BEYOND A REASONABLE DOUBT

EVIDENCE FOR CHRISTIANITY

THIRD EDITION

Terry Siciliano

Scripture quotations not designated are from 'The Holy Bible: New International Version', copyright 1973, 1978, 1984 by the International Bible Society, Published by Zondervan Bible Publishers, Grand Rapids Michigan.

Other translations are designated as follows:
ESV The English Standard Version
NKJV The New King James Version
TLB The Living Bible

Beyond a Reasonable Doubt:
Evidence for Christianity

Published by Truth Press
Chester, Maryland
First printing 2000
Revised (2nd) edition) 2001
Revised (3rd edition) 2020

Printed in the United States of America

ISBN: 0-9710199-5-9

Cover design by bookcovers.com

This book is for all who sincerely want to know
the one, true God.

It is for the poor in spirit,
those who mourn,
the meek,
those who hunger and thirst for righteousness,
the merciful,
pure in heart,
peacemakers,
those who are persecuted for righteousness sake.
For theirs is the kingdom of heaven
and they shall see God.
(Matthew 5:6-10)

To my best friend and husband Dave,
my children Brittany and Kelly,
my son-in-law Eric, and my granddaughter Kayla.
You have all brightened my world more than you know.
May God bless you richly until He comes.

TABLE OF CONTENTS

Preface

This special edition was inspired by chaotic events occurring around the world today and its purpose is to give hope, confidence, and peace to those anxious about the future. Jesus gave us signs that would precede His Second Coming to Earth, often termed "The End Times," and He used the analogy of a woman in labor having contractions prior to the birth of a child. Each pang would be painful and increase in intensity and frequency as the time approached. Some signs of the end include the escalation of natural disasters, wars, famine, disease, corruption, injustice, greed, lust, poverty, fear, false religions, self-centeredness, hatred, evil, confusion, uncertainty, panic, terror, rebellious children, high divorce and suicide rates, and a general disbelief in God.

As I type these words, a new strain of coronavirus called COVID-19 ravages the globe infecting millions and killing hundreds of thousands. Governments have responded by issuing stay-at-home orders, closing businesses, churches, sporting events, schools, concerts, casinos, beaches, parks, and any place people tend to gather in groups. Graduations, weddings, reunions, and even funerals are among many of the life events that have either been canceled or postponed. People are required to wear masks in public places and avoid contact with others while the elderly are quarantined in nursing homes and assisted living facilities where their families are prohibited from visiting. Individuals are losing their livelihoods, unemployment is skyrocketing, and national economies are being crushed. Calls to suicide prevention hot lines have increased over 800 percent this year. Airports are empty, subways are filled with the homeless, and public transportation is extremely limited. Times Square, the Vatican, Rodeo Drive, and even Disney World are deserted. All 50 of the United States of America are under disaster declaration for first time in the country's history because of the pandemic.

Amidst the virus, a separate event has sparked riots and protests in over 400 American cities and many others around the world. The chaos was prompted by the actions of a white police officer who, during an arrest, caused the horrifying death of a black man named George Floyd while other officers simply looked on. An outraged crowd observed the despicable scene and worldwide protests have erupted. The U.S. National Guard has recently been deployed in many areas because of looting, vicious attacks on police forces, and the burning of private and government property, even American flags. Rage-filled mobs are throwing broken bottles, bricks, and firebombs at people trying to protect the public while innocent store owners are being severely beaten or killed trying to defend their businesses. Recently, the President of the United States was whisked into a secure bunker beneath the White House by Secret Service agents because of the extreme violence while individuals vandalized the Lincoln, WWII, and other precious memorials in Washington D.C. Prominent statues from America's history are being defaced, toppled, or removed from their sites. Each night, cities burn and curfews are put in place. The U.S. is in a crisis and its leaders cower in fear offering no solutions. People around the globe are furious and totally fed up with entrenched racism and are denouncing police brutality while demanding major reforms. The labor pains of this world do indeed appear to be intensifying and multiplying at increasing speed.

For those who are suffering, grieving, and fearful, this message is for you.

Hope and peace can be found, by belief and trust in Jesus Christ, the Savior of the world. Disease, death, and suffering entered the world because of man's rebellion against God. Jesus is called the Savior because He came to Earth to rescue men gripped by sin and evil and He offers forgiveness and eternal life to those who put their faith and trust in Him. He taught that there is more beyond this world and that hell and heaven, are real places for those who will either be judged for their actions or receive mercy despite them. Jesus was cruelly and unjustly crucified, died on a cross in Jerusalem, and then proved He has power over death by rising from the grave. That is the Gospel message: the future of all who place their faith and trust in Him are secure no matter what happens in this life or how grim things may appear. Those who follow Christ are given a fresh start, promised a new life, and will ultimately be given a body which will never die. Jesus even promises to restore the earth where one day there will be no more sin, death, mourning, crying, or pain. In the meantime, we can have a Father who loves us deeply, empathizes with our suffering, and answers our pleas for help through prayer. And if our loved ones believed, we can know we will never be separated permanently from them.

This book was my quest to discover the truth about God, whether the Bible can be trusted, who Jesus claimed to be, if there is credible evidence for the claims and promises of the Christian faith and if so, then a person can follow Jesus with unshakable confidence and have peace in this uncertain world while looking forward to the next. He said this about the end times: "Peace I leave with you; my peace I give to you… Let not your hearts be troubled, neither let them be afraid… I have told you before it takes place, so that when it does take place, you may believe" John 14:27-29 (ESV). Jesus offers peace, comfort, safety, and a sure future for those who love, follow, believe in Him, and accept His gift of salvation that was bought with His own precious blood. His death and suffering in our place is truly remarkable and that extreme act of kindness should be thoughtfully considered and explored. I pray this book will provide some of the answers for those who wonder whether or not God exists and if He provided a remedy for this broken world.

-Terry Siciliano
May 2020

Introduction

It was never my intention to write a book and it was the furthest thing from my mind. It began as an intense compilation of notes during an arduous journey toward an unknown destination. When this journey began I was very happily married to the person I considered my best friend and soul mate. We had two beautiful children, successful and satisfying careers, our dream home that we had built together, and a life that was just grand. Then suddenly, after about eight years of marriage, our road became quite rocky and we couldn't seem to get along. We still loved each other but didn't really like each other very much. Our kids were sad and confused and we did not know how to fix things between us. Both of us had been raised Catholic and knew *about* God but didn't really *know* God. Growing up we each went through all the motions and rituals of being religious, but it was more robotic in nature than spiritual.

Ten years prior to meeting my future husband, I attended college. During my freshman year, with help from my roommate, I learned what it meant to have a personal relationship with Jesus Christ. However, for lack of nourishment and fellowship with other believers, my new-found faith at that time came under attack and began to weaken. I was majoring in the sciences, which excluded God from the world. I then drifted slowly away from Christianity for quite a long period as I pursued and established my career. I became an Air Force pilot, where I met my husband, and we were both eventually hired by different airlines. I spent a year in the first Gulf War, then had our two girls, moved and built a house. It was a busy, yet exciting time, filled with stress and that is when things began to go wrong.

Some years later, a friend crossed my path and said that if I knew God as he did, that He would not only help us regain what we had lost but make it infinitely better. I scoffed a bit at this, but I faintly remembered my previous relationship with the Lord. This friend gave me a book similar to the one you are now reading. My education had nearly convinced me that the universe did not have a cause nor a beginning, that life on Earth sprouted from a swamp of chemical compounds, and that I was descended from apes. According to others, there was no reason to believe in a Creator since science had all of the answers and excluded Him. Some doubts still tugged at the edges of my mind such as, how can something come from nothing, why are we even here, is there any purpose to life, if there is no moral code for which we are responsible, then why do I have a guilty conscience when I do bad things, and of course, why has my marriage taken this turn for the worse and what is the solution?

I began to study more closely the theories of the origins of the universe, evolution, and the likelihood that life could be generated spontaneously without an intelligent agent behind it all. As I poured over book after book, I learned how incredibly complex even a single living cell is at the microbiological level, how precisely ordered was the universe and planet Earth, and that there is no evidence at all in the fossil record of macroevolution (the theory that species evolve into other, different species). There should be abundant evidence in the geological strata if that were true. If I were to reconsider that perhaps a good God was the intelligent architect behind the created world then His inspired Word recorded by faithful servants must contain the truth. The turning point then, for me, was after reading the first pages of Genesis and concluding that someone was giving me incomplete, and at times false, information.

I read the entire Bible for the first time, started bringing our girls to church, listened to sermons and studies on the radio, and asked that friend of mine lots of questions about God. I learned that it was our own sin that was getting in between my husband and me. I began looking in the mirror for what it was that *I* was doing to make him unkind toward me instead of always blaming our problems on him. I tried to be more loving, attentive, supportive, appreciative and learned to say, "I'm sorry." Man's pride is the root of all kinds of evil. Love is supposed to be patient and kind, not proud, envious, boastful, arrogant, rude, irritable, or resentful. Neither does it insist on its own way (1 Corinthians 13:4).

My notes were really piling up and I typed them into a 75 page report that I snuck into my husband's luggage prior to one of his trips. You see, my initial motivation for this effort was to convince him of what I now believed, that God was real and that scientific explanations for the world and beyond were totally inadequate. The evidence for God certainly tipped the scales in my opinion. I began to pray fervently for him, us, and our relationship and He answered those prayers. My husband ultimately became a believer and after both of us put our trust in Christ we began to see how He had originally intended the husband and wife relationship to be. When we began treating each other with more mutual respect, love, less self-centeredness and more compassion, things began to change. We now have over 31 years in our relationship and it has never been better or stronger. What you have here are my notes, organized into readable material, edited and updated to include some recent discoveries made in the areas of science and archaeology since the first publication over twenty years ago.

I never became a scientist but I do have a Bachelor of Science in the field of Physical Science. I have been a pilot for over thirty years with the world's largest airline, and as a captain, I am an analytical thinker and problem solver highly trained to prioritize and execute appropriate procedures in any given situation which results in making timely life or death decisions. Up to 225 souls are in my hands at any given moment and all persons on any given flight are relying on me and my crew to always make the right call as situations arise.

Each of us has a unique circle of individuals whom we influence during the course of our life and some, specifically our closest family members, rely on us to properly analyze our view of the world and pass it on to the very best of our ability. This world view should include our consideration of spiritual things when asked our opinion regarding life's most probing questions. Those inevitably come from the children we raise and it is a high calling indeed to give reasonable and well thought out answers. Therefore, I have considered it my duty as a responsible parent to seek the truth.

I feel a person should base his or her beliefs on reasonable evidence *and* personal experience instead of hearsay which does take a considerable amount of homework. I do not believe we should rely simply on what we have been told even from well meaning parents, friends, spiritual advisors, colleagues and others. This is most important to me in all areas of my life, and not just the spiritual. For example, if I have a financial investment strategy, it had better be based on some serious research. There is a lot at stake when my spouse and I are planning our retirement or our children's future education. We do our due diligence first using all available data and don't simply rely on any one person's advice. Normally, we would insist on a prospectus as proof of past performance for a mutual fund, follow the business section of the paper, review investment magazines and portfolios, etc. If one of our children became seriously ill, we would seek out the most respected and experienced doctors, find a specialized hospital, and read the most current medical journals dealing with the illness before making an ultimate decision for treatment.

All of us can approach questions regarding spirituality in the exact same manner. After all, lives are at stake, so why wouldn't we? Some people may disagree with my methods and motivation and think an individual's spiritual beliefs should be strictly private and based on a simple, trusting, and even blind faith; I emphatically disagree. It is my belief that God exists and made us rational, thinking human beings. He also chose to give us the gift of free will and intellect whereby we retain dignity, honor, and autonomy. Ultimately, the decision to accept or reject Him is solely ours to make. I don't think any of us should take that lightly and that it is everyone's responsibility to seek the truth earnestly and with determination, using all available resources.

Finding the truth for myself has involved a considerable amount of research, but has been well worth the effort as I am entirely satisfied with the answers that I have found. While there are certainly ways to attempt to explain away the abundant evidence for Christianity, we have to ask ourselves, "What is the most *reasonable* explanation for the evidence that we have?" Faith should not just be a blind "feeling" but a real trust in something or *someone* precisely because of the evidence before us. Evidence leads to knowing which, in turn, leads us to putting our trust in that knowledge. What one needs to decide is whether there is sufficient evidence beyond a reasonable doubt that God is real and proceed from there. The sole purpose of this writing is simply to share information I have discovered during my research and to share it with others who are seeking truth for themselves. What follows are not my own ideas, but rather, verifiable, historic and scientific facts and the conclusions I have drawn based on those facts. My prayer is that whoever reads this will continue to search further and probe deeper toward finding satisfactory answers to some of life's most difficult questions.

1

Evidence From Creation

There is such abundant evidence in the known universe, in our solar system, and on our privileged planet which is uniquely suited to sustain life, that the creation must have had a designer. In addition to scientist's final conclusion that the universe had a beginning, I believe the incredible complexities we find in all three logically rule out random formation even as a remote possibility. There is virtually zero evidence in the geologic record of life evolving from non-living chemicals nor across species including from ape to man. The theist (one who believes in God), believes the account recorded in the first sentence of the Bible and that "God created the heavens and the earth," and then every species of plant and creature. During the Cambrian Period most major animal species made their first, grand appearance in the fossil record. This clearly supports the biblical account and not the gradual development evolutionists theorize. There is also geologic evidence of a widespread flood which is recorded in Genesis, chapter seven. Finally, if there is no God and we are all simply a mass of random molecules, then we have no grounds for a godly moral code, do not need to answer to a higher power, and human life has little value. We can certainly see where this type of thinking has led, considering the thoughtless, heartless killings that occur on a daily basis throughout the world.

THE UNIVERSE

If an intelligent Being created the universe at a specific point in time, then we should be able to see some evidence of this in the cosmos. Indeed we have and it fits with the most widely accepted theory for the beginning of the universe: The Big Bang. Using the laws of physics, it is the model that describes the explosion and expansion of the universe from a single point.

Einstein's theory of General Relativity has now been proven accurate beyond doubt and reveals there was a definite beginning to all time, matter, and space. It predicted the universe was expanding which was later observed by Edwin Hubble and has been confirmed. The Law of Causality states that everything has a cause and is the fundamental principle of all science. Therefore, if the universe had a beginning, then it must have had a cause and the First Law of Thermodynamics insists that something cannot come from nothing. The Second Law of Thermodynamics states that matter and energy are expended over time as disorder increases. So the universe had a cause and a beginning, and expands today and as it does it is running out of energy. Theists believe that God was the initiator since again, something cannot come from nothing.

All celestial bodies are moving apart from one another. This was first observed in 1927 by astronomer Edwin Hubble (namesake of the space telescope). It was later confirmed when Arno Penzias and Robert Wilson won the Nobel Prize in 1978 after they detected cosmic microwave background radiation which is an afterglow of light and heat in the cosmos at Bell Labs, in Holmdel, New Jersey in 1965. This phenomenon would have to be present if the universe began with an initial explosion.

Agnostic astronomer Robert Jastrow put it this way,

> No explanation other than the Big Bang has been found for the fireball radiation. The clincher, which has convinced almost the last doubting Thomas, is that the radiation discovered by Penzias and Wilson has exactly the pattern of wavelengths expected for the light and heat produced in a great explosion. Others have tried desperately to find an alternative explanation, but they have failed. At the present time, the Big Bang theory has no competitors.[1]

The question one needs to be asking is, "Who created this matter and who caused the 'Big Bang' in the first place?" The first words written in the Bible are, "In the beginning, God created the heavens and the earth." Then it describes the filling and forming of that universe with things like light, darkness, water, seas, land, vegetation, creatures and lastly, man. This description in Genesis, the first book of the Bible, fits perfectly with the Big Bang Theory.

U.S. News and World Report printed an article on July 20, 1998, which states,

> The issue of what caused the universe has often been one the science world would rather skip... Researchers have calculated that after a big bang, unless the ratio of matter to energy to the volume of the universe, (a value researchers call "omega"), was within one quadrillionth of one percent of the ideal, runaway relativity would have rendered the cosmos uninhabitable: either too scrunched and distorted for life, or too diffuse for stars to form... Had gravity been only slightly stronger, stars would burn through their nuclear fuel in less than a year: life could never evolve, much less settle in. Had the strong force that holds nuclear atoms together been only slightly weaker, stars could never have formed. So far, no theory is even close to explaining why physical laws exist, much less why they take the form they do. Standard big-bang theory, for example, essentially explains the propitious universe in this way: "Well, we got lucky."
>
> A conference in Berkeley, California, at which cosmologists discussed the theological implications of their work, is representative. Allan Sandage, one of the world's leading astronomers, told the gathering that contemplating the majesty

> of the big bang helped make him a believer in God, willing to accept that creation could only be explained as a miracle. Not that long ago, such a comment from an established scientist would have been shocking. Today, intellectuals are beginning to find it respectable to talk about how physical law seems to favor life. The unknown of the big bang eventually will be seen as divine latency. The theological idea of creation ex nihilio - out of nothing - is looking better all the time as theories increasingly suggest the universe emerged from no tangible source.

Christian apologist and blogger, Laura Z. Powell writes that the universe, our solar system, and our planet are precisely and perfectly suited to support life and were designed by a designer and lists the following evidences for the design argument:

- If the universe had expanded at a rate one millionth more slowly than it did, the universe would have collapsed on itself; any faster, and no galaxies would have formed.
- If the centrifugal force of planetary movements did not precisely balance the gravitational forces, nothing could be held in orbit around the sun.
- If the gravitational force were altered by 0.0000 000000000000000000000000000000001 percent, our sun would not exist.

- If Jupiter's gravitational field did not act as a vacuum cleaner to attract asteroids and comets, Earth would be bombarded with these fatal objects.

EARTH

- If the thickness of the Earth's crust were greater, too much oxygen would be transferred to the crust to support life; if thinner, volcanic and tectonic activity would make life impossible.
- If the 23-degree axial tilt of the Earth were altered slightly, surface temperatures would be too extreme for life.
- If Earth's rotation took more than 24 hours, temperature differences would be too great between night & day; if less time, atmospheric wind velocities would be too great.
  - If there was more seismic activity, a lot more life would be lost; if less, nutrients on the ocean floors and in river runoff would not be cycled back to the continents through tectonic uplift (yes, even earthquakes are necessary for life!)
  - If rates of lightning were greater, there would be too much fire destruction; if less, there would be too little nitrogen fixing in the soil.
  - If water vapor levels in the atmosphere were greater, a runaway greenhouse effect would cause temperatures to rise too high for human life; if

less, an insufficient greenhouse effect would make Earth too cold for human life.

- If the ratio of the gravitational force to the electromagnetic force were altered by less than one part in 10^{40} (one in ten thousand trillion trillion trillion), life would not exist.

She quotes astrophysicist Hugh Ross who said, "The odds that any planet in the universe would possess the necessary conditions to support intelligent physical life is less than one in (10^{173}), a number so large that it might as well be infinity."[2]

Powell concludes that, "The more that is discovered about the universe, the more evident it is that our universe was designed on purpose with human life in mind. Every design, every purpose, and every mind proceeds from an intelligent being. The complexity of design in the universe most assuredly points to a magnificently intelligent and powerful Designer." [3]

LIFE

The earth's ecosystems also work together in perfect harmony and now that we've shown the argument for a designed and created universe and planet suited to support life, let us explore life itself and the odds that it could be generated accidentally and without an intelligent agent behind it.

The evolutionist explains that the chance development of life began on earth with an unusual chemical mixture they call the "primordial" or "prebiotic" soup that spontaneously generated life from nonliving material. I find the imagery amusing that all of life's incredibly complex forms originated with a grand batch of soup! Since the evolutionist rejects the possibility of a supernatural designer, he is forced to accept the only other available alternative: random chance.

Professor Chandra Wickramasinghe, an eminent British scientist, concluded:

> The earth's atmosphere was never the right character to form an organic soup… it doesn't follow that if you have an organic soup it could get life started… And when we looked at the probabilities of the assembly of organic materials into a living system, it turns out that the improbabilities are really horrendous, horrific in extent and could not have happened spontaneously on the earth.…There's not enough time, there's not enough resources and there's no way in which that could have happened on the earth.[4]

Biologists have calculated the actual odds against this spontaneous generation of life are one chance in 10 to the 40,000th power. To put this in perspective, scientists have calculated the number of atoms existing in our universe is only 10 to the 74th power.[5]

Microbiologist Michael Denton, a proclaimed atheist, has said, "The complexity of the simplest known type of cell is so great that it is impossible to accept that such an object could have been thrown together suddenly by some kind of freakish, vastly improbable event. Such an occurrence would be indistinguishable from a miracle."[6]

He is absolutely correct. Now that we have the ability to view and explore the inside of a cell, its complexity baffles the mind. Living things are filled with molecular machines that are irreducibly complex and all parts of it must be precisely ordered for the machine to function. Michael Behe writes, "The results of these cumulative efforts to investigate the cell-to investigate life at the molecular level-is a loud, clear, piercing cry of 'design!' The result is so ambiguous and so significant that it must be ranked as one of the greatest achievements in the history of science."[7]

DNA is the chemical that encodes instructions for building living things and is so complex that within every human cell there consists 3,000 million pairs of the genetic alphabet and their sequence within a living cell determines a person's unique genetic makeup. A human has trillions of these cells. A single celled amoeba contains as much information as 1,000 sets of the Encyclopedia Britannica, so imagine how much information is stored in trillions of cells. The DNA contains the instructions that precisely order the amino acids in the proteins for the cell to function properly. It is impossible for that to happen randomly.

COMPLEX ORGANS

The complexity of organs in any living creature is another evidence for the design argument. The human body is a masterpiece of cells, systems, and chemistry all working together in beautiful harmony. The Bible says that we are "fearfully and wonderfully made" and that our parts were "intricately woven" into a beautiful, unified whole (Psalm 139:14-15).

Let us view one fabulous example: the human eye.

Apologist Grant Jeffrey writes, "When we marvel at the profound complexity of the human eye, for example, one must conclude that it is highly unlikely that it has evolved over millions of years by many, random chance mutations. The retina cells perform up to ten billion calculations per second to determine the image transmitted to the eye by light photons."[8]

Dr. John Stevens made this startling comparison in an article published by *Byte* computer magazine in their April 1985 issue:

> If we were to attempt to duplicate the computing power of the human eye, we would have to build the world's most advanced computer with a single silicon chip (normally the size of a dime) that

> would cover 10,000 cubic inches and contain billions of transistors and hundreds of miles of circuit traces. The retina is so small that it fills only 0.0003 inches of space...the computer chip would weigh at least 100 pounds, in comparison to the human retina that weighs less than a gram. The retina operates with less than 0.0001 watts of electrical charge. To duplicate the retina's abilities, the computer would need to consume 300 watts of power. In other words, the retina is 3,000,000 times more efficient in its power consumption.
>
> Charles Darwin actually admitted that the engineering of the human eye was so specialized and complex that he could not begin to imagine how it might have developed through the evolutionary processes of random mutation and natural selection.[9]
>
> He stated: "To suppose that the eye with all its inimitable contrivances for adjusting the focus to different distances, for admitting different amounts of light, and for the correction of spherical and chromatic aberration, could have been formed by natural selection, seems, I freely confess, absurd in the highest degree."[10]

These statements are incredible and shows that Darwin seriously questioned his own theory.

It is difficult to imagine how, not just the eye, but all of the complex organs found in men and animals could have possibly been formed through chance mutations. It is also significant that not one new species of plant or animal is known to have evolved on Earth during recorded history.

Who is to say that the scientist's study and observation of the fascinating workings of biology, astronomy, chemistry, meteorology, and geology are not simply man's study of God's handiwork? Many famous scientists who were Christians had found it quite reasonable to reconcile science with the Bible. Just three examples are Johannes Kepler, Isaac Newton, and Louis Pasteur.

EVOLUTION

Let's move on from the impossibility of living cells to form by random chance to the theory that all living creatures descended from a first, single celled organism and all of that was done "naturally" thus the term, "natural selection. "Darwin's Theory of Evolution is taught as fact in the education system but people do not realize that the theory is built upon evidence of micro evolution which refers to small evolutionary changes *within* a species or population while macro evolution is evolution on a scale of separated gene pools. Microevolution is supported by the fossil evidence but there is absolutely no evidence for macroevolution which is the belief that all life forms have descended from a common ancestor. In other words, microevolution may be able to explain the survival of a species because of slight changes within a species adapting to the environment, but it cannot explain the arrival of a new species.

There are more than three million existing species of insects and thousands of species of mammals, reptiles, and birds. For evolution to be true, every one of these species would have needed to overcome the overwhelming odds against random chance formation. It should be obvious that the origin of millions of separate species cannot be explained by the theory of evolution.

Natural selection requires progressive development of species, yet in the fossil record we never find animals whose parts are incompletely formed. How could a heart function at all, for example, if formed in gradual and incomplete stages? Unless it was formed perfectly functional in the first place, it would be of absolutely no use. Charles Darwin optimistically predicted that eventually, fossils would be found to prove his theory and if correct, the geological stratum should be loaded with fossils exhibiting innumerable transitional forms which would lend credence to his theory. These layers should contain at least a sampling of the 'missing link' fossils, which show mutations representing a continuum of change. Despite millions of paleontologists and amateurs searching for examples during the last 170 years, none have been found.

Dr. Stephen Jay Gould, the Professor of Geology and Paleontology at Harvard University, admits that the evidence from the fossil record thus far does not support evolution. He wrote the following statement in an article for *Natural History* magazine (May 1997, p.14):

> The extreme rarity of transitional forms in the fossil record persists as the trade secret of paleontology. The evolutionary trees that adorn our textbooks have data only at the tips and nodes of their branches; the rest is inference, however reasonable, not the evidence of fossils. Yet Darwin was so wedded to gradualism that he wagered his entire theory on a denial of this literal record:
>
> "The geological record is extremely imperfect and this fact will to a large extent explain why we do not find interminable varieties, connecting together all the extinct and existing forms of life by the finest graduated steps. He who rejects these views on the nature of the geological record, will rightly reject my whole theory."...We view our data as so bad that we never see the very process we profess to study.

At a molecular level there is no trace of the evolutionary transition from fish to amphibian, or from reptile to mammal. So amphibia, always traditionally considered intermediate between fish and the other terrestrial vertebrates, are in molecular terms as far from fish as any group of reptiles or mammals! To those well acquainted

> with the traditional picture of vertebrate evolution the result is truly astonishing.[11]

Even the oldest fossils that have been found show definition, which gives no indication of evolving biological parts. Sedimentary layers containing examples of existing and extinct organisms have clearly defined gaps between them where the evolutionist would expect to find transitional forms, yet none have been found. It would appear that the organisms were formed perfectly from the beginning. This is precisely what one would expect if the Bible's account of creation were true.

THE FLOOD

While on the topic of the fossil record, does it indicate evidence of the flood described in Genesis? A catastrophic event of such gigantic proportions would certainly yield evidences preserved in the geologic columns and that is exactly what we find: graveyards filled with fossils likely preserved by a dramatic and rapid deposition of sediments. Yet scientists claim that the average rate of sedimentary deposition during the last geologic epoch (the Pleistocene), was only .024 inches per year.[12]

If that is so, then why were an estimated eight hundred million skeletons of Vertebrate animals found in the Karroo formation in South Africa? The Monterrey shale contains over a billion fossil fish covering four square miles.[13]

Is it more believable that slow deposition preserved these fossils or that it was the result of the large flood described in the Bible? The fossils found include the outline of entire fish, not just the bones. A lobster fossil in Germany was found where it was apparently in the act of catching a small fish.[14]

A slab of sandstone found in New York has preserved over 400 starfish, some of which died hovering over clams they were in the process of devouring. [15] Fossilized animal footprints are not even uncommon. The Coconino footprints found in Arizona are in sandstone (which would indicate a dune deposit) and interestingly, they almost always run uphill.[16] Could they have been possibly trying to escape rising floodwaters?

FROM APE TO MAN?

The Theory of Evolution has some very serious flaws and, as we will see, the theory is finally collapsing due to the total absence of evidence in its favor. The fossils paleontologists use to 'prove' that Homo sapiens came from apes often consist of merely a tooth, piece of jawbone, or elbow joint. The textbook illustrators have created an entire human being out of a single tooth. Many times, the hominid fossil skeletons have been pieced together with fragments that were found over several miles.

Some examples of hominid fossil hoaxes are the Piltdown Man, where someone had placed a human skullcap on top of an ape's jawbone and this had been considered a legitimate discovery for fifty years! Another example is Ramapithecus, which was supposedly the missing link between man and apes for another fifty years and based on a single tooth that later turned out to be indeed the tooth from a modern orangutan. A third example is the Neanderthal Man, which turned out to be the fossil of a modern man who had suffered a deficiency of vitamin D that had produced rickets. This disease accounted for the slumped shoulders, curved leg bones, and ridges over the eyebrows. The Nebraska Man and his wife were illustrated on the covers of prestigious magazines worldwide. These two characters had been constructed from a single tooth, which turned out to be the tooth of an extinct pig! [17]

The famous Dr. Richard Leakey stated:

> Our task is not unlike attempting to assemble a three dimensional jigsaw puzzle in which most of the pieces are missing, and those few bits which are at hand are broken!" Dr. Gareth Nelson of the American Museum of Natural History exclaimed, "We've got to have some ancestors. We'll pick those. Why? Because we know they have to be there, and these are the best candidates. That's by and large the way it has worked. I am not exaggerating.[18]

There have been twelve hominoid fossils found which are the supposed 'missing links' that 'prove' man has evolved from apes. Nine of those have been proven to be apes while the remaining three have proven to be modern humans; they are Homo Erectus, Neanderthal Man, and Cro Magnon Man. Homo Erectus was thought to be an ape only because of his small brain. It has recently been proven that his brain is the same size as the average European man's brain. Neanderthal Man turned out to be a man with rickets disease. Cro Magnon Man was thought to be ape-like merely because he was found near a series of caves, which had drawings that were considered primitive. Evolutionary scientists have failed to find a single genuine transitional form between apes and men despite their constant search during the last 170 years.

The teaching of Darwin's Theory of Evolution in the public schools as 'fact', combined with the prohibition of teaching creation as a 'possibility' is utterly unfair as neither has been proven. It would be more appropriate for students to be exposed to this theory as well as the biblical account of creation. It would also be fitting to reveal the evidence that is contrary to Darwin's theory.

MATERIALISM

A popular view of man and his world is one called 'materialism' where matter is the only reality; the totality of your personality is simply the function of your biological system acting and reacting in a social context. It is one where all in the universe is reducible to matter and can be explained in terms of physical laws. This means that thought and love are material or chemical and nothing more. It also teaches that we have no soul, there is no afterlife, we will not be held accountable for our life, and thus, we have no purpose. However, Jean Piaget, the ultimate child psychologist, tells us that man naturally believes that there is purpose to the world. The psychologist Victor Frankl argues that the need for purpose or meaning is man's *most basic* need.

Materialism cannot justify any concept of right and wrong nor have any room for a moral code. According to materialism, man is not different from other beings and cannot be considered a 'responsible agent.' It does not allow for a soul but that man is simply a product of his genes or environment.

In the theistic view, man is the image-bearer of God who possesses a soul which permits him to know the moral law and enables him to say 'no' to the influences from his genes and/or environment if he so desires. In theism man can be described as a moral agent responsible for his own actions. Materialism describes man as the product of material forces which determine why he acts as he does and as if there is nothing he can do about it. In this view, we lose the basis for determining a healthy self-esteem which is grounded in truth, and substitute an unhealthy one where one merely 'feels good' about himself.[19]

In this view, there are really few, if any, choices for a man to make and because of this, I am surprised it is so popular today. Aren't we individuals free to make our own choices? Maybe the materialist hasn't totally thought this concept through. As individuals, then, we would be without any worth or purpose at all.

God's Word explains that He created man with the moral code written on our hearts and as if that weren't enough, God himself even engraved His laws on stone tablets which were first entrusted to the Israelites. The materialist is committed to scientism, the belief that all knowledge must pass the test of scientific evidence and that it is the only thing that contains 'truth.' It has been the predominant model in our educational system. Hence, to oppose posting the Ten Commandments on a courtroom wall or to prohibit teaching in public schools that God may have created the universe is to disguise private preference with 'public' truth.

Isn't it wrong to impose one's tastes on others in a free society? Recently, the intent of separation of church and state has changed from "freedom of religion" to "freedom from religion." But isn't materialism itself a religious view? What has been the result of teaching this publicly 'acceptable' view? If we are simply the chemical and biological products of our environment with no moral code, soul, or purpose and are not accountable for our actions, how will our children and future generations handle this knowledge? The result can already be seen; many youths today have no hope for the future and are in total despair. As a result, the teenage suicide rate in America is the highest it has ever been. Children murdering other children was practically non-existent a generation ago, yet how many of these incidences have occurred the past few years in our country alone? Violent crime, especially among teenagers, is at an all time high. Is it really better to suppress knowledge of God, or would it be in our children's best interest to teach both views, theistic and non-theistic, which include all known evidence, and let each decide for themselves what is true and what is not?

One would have to admit that is indeed a weak argument to explain the perfect harmony that can be seen in the earth's ecosystems, solar system, and the human body are the result of an accident. It is a far greater leap of faith to believe this harmony is by chance than it is to believe in a creator. The mathematical odds against the idea that all we see in creation is simply the result of an accident are enormous.

2

The Background of The Bible

Most people think of the Bible as one book but it is actually a library of 66 books written by some 40 authors over a period of approximately 1,500 years. Having been written by so many different people with very diverse backgrounds, its unity and harmony is a miracle in itself.

The Protestant Bible has two major parts: The Old Testament (or Hebrew Bible) and The New Testament. The Old Testament contains 39 books and is referred to as "Scripture" in the New Testament. The first five books (called the Torah) begin with Genesis and are believed to have been written by Moses in approximately 1400 BC. Genesis describes the creation of the universe and the start of the human race. It then continues with the history of God's chosen people — Abraham, Isaac, Jacob, and their descendants, whom God formed into the nation of Israel.

In the Old Testament, God begins to show his plan for man and that He gave us a free will to obey Him or rebel against Him. It explains the origin and definition of sin, which is to disobey God and place your own personal desires above His. Man's first sin resulted in separation from God's presence and initiated suffering, sickness, and death in the world. Through God's chosen prophets (those individuals who received direct revelations from God), He promised to send a Messiah, the Savior of sinners and the means by which all can be a part of God's eternal kingdom.

The New Testament is believed to have been completed by around 90 AD. (Note: BC means "before Christ" and AD means "Anno Domini" which translates as "In the year of our Lord"). There are 27 books in the New Testament which include the written accounts of Jesus' life, the formation of the Christian Church, and a revelation of things to come. The first four books: Matthew, Mark, Luke, and John, contain Christ's teachings during His earthly ministry and are called the "Gospels." Jesus gave the disciples the task of starting the Christian Church by spreading the good news of salvation and giving living testimony of all He did. By the way, the term disciple means student, so they were disciples while Jesus lived on Earth and taught them. They became Apostles, which means messenger, after Jesus ascended to heaven.

Acts is the book that follows the four Gospels and includes the "acts" of the Apostles following Jesus' resurrection. This book describes their travels and how they founded the Christian Church. Its primary purpose was to instruct the people and involve them in the spread of the Gospel message. Acts is followed by letters written by various Apostles to the newly founded churches and the last book is Revelation, which describes Christ's return and the end of the world. Described in detail are the new heaven and the new earth, which will be created, and the final fall of Satan.

The Old Testament was originally written in Hebrew and Aramaic. About 250 years before Jesus' birth, it was translated into Greek (the largest world civilization at the time). Three hundred and fifty years after Jesus' death, it was translated into Latin (the common language at that time). This translation was called the Vulgate and was the official Bible in Western Europe for over 1,000 years.

The first English translation was prepared in the late 1300's. Since the printing press had not been invented, all copies were transcribed by hand (an extremely tedious process), and very few were available. It wasn't until 1440 that the first English Bible was printed on a press. Many more English translations have been made since. The purpose of these translations is that they are written in the language and style that people speak today which makes understanding God's message much easier. Please do not equate translation with inaccuracy. The message is perfectly intact and has been meticulously recorded and translated into over 3,500 other languages.

The Bible has only been in mass production during the last few centuries and in light of this history I feel very fortunate not only to own a Bible, but also to have so many different translations available to read and study. God has told us that a sign of the end times is that the Gospel would be spread to all nations in every tongue and that knowledge would increase. We are certainly approaching fulfillment of those prophecies since Bibles are now available in nearly every world language.

ARCHAEOLOGY

Recent archeological discoveries have continued to verify the Bible's credibility in terms of its reliability as an accurate portrayer of historical events, kings, ancient cities, and the life of Christ. In fact, none of the findings contradict the biblical historic record, they only continue to support it. To date, 24,633 ancient New Testament manuscripts have been found and documented. This is far more than any other ancient historical work.[20] And although we don't have the original documents, the thousands that have been documented and examined confirm the accuracy of the New Testament that we have today.

The Old Testament contains detailed information about past events, kings, nations, wars, geography, customs, economics, politics, and more. To consider the Bible as an accurate, historical work, one would look to archeology to determine some of its credibility. It so happens that there has been an explosion of archeological knowledge in the last 150 years which has provided ample evidence, even for the most determined skeptic, that the Bible can be trusted as an accurate portrayer of historic events. We will examine just a few examples of writings that have been found on ancient materials which substantiate the history that is recorded in the Bible.

> Excavations at Nazi, Mari, and Alalakh provide background information that fits well with the Genesis stories of the patriarchal period [the time of Israel's founding fathers]...The Ebla tablets recently discovered in northern Syria also affirm the antiquity and accuracy of the Book of Genesis...The biblical description of the Hittite empire was confirmed...when the Hittite capital was discovered in 1906....Other excavations agree with the account in Joshua about the conquest of Canaan and shed light on the period of the Judges and the reigns of Saul and David.... Excavations at Hazor, Gezer, Megiddo, and Jerusalem and Phoenician inscriptions illuminate Solomon's reign.
>
> The Moabite Stone yields information about the reign of Omri, the sixth King of Israel. The Black Obelisk of Shalmaneser III depicts how King Jehu of Israel had to submit to the Assyrian King. The Taylor Prism has an Assyrian text which describes Sennacherib's siege of Jerusalem when Hezekiah was king. The Lachish Letters refer to Nebuchadnezzar's invasion of Judah and illustrate the life and times of Jeremiah the prophet.[21]

The Pool of Siloam where Jesus healed a blind man was found in 2004. The ossuary (a limestone box), holding the bones of Caiaphas, the High Priest who presided over Jesus' trial, was found in 1990. The "Pilate Stone" found in 1961 confirms that Pontius Pilate was the governor of Judea when Jesus was handed over by him to be crucified. The Assyrian Limmu List Tablet allows us to date over 250 years of Assyrian history which coincides with the history of Israel recorded in the Old Testament. The Cyrus Cylinder confirms the biblical claims that King Cyrus allowed the Israelites to return to their homeland after the Babylonian captivity and rebuild their temple.

TRANSCRIPTION AND PRESERVATION

Many people have difficulty believing in the authenticity of the Bible because it has been translated so many times and is thousands of years old. I have learned that the translators of the Bible have meticulously preserved the original writings and have gone to extraordinary measures to faithfully preserve its meaning. No other book ever written has undergone more continuous inspection and scrutiny and I believe the following evidence more than adequately proves that the Bible's content has been preserved with incredible accuracy throughout the years.

THE DEAD SEA SCROLLS

In 1947 an Arab shepherd boy found some very old papyrus papers covered in writing which have since been named the Dead Sea Scrolls. This has been called perhaps the greatest archeological discovery in the history of the world. These writings have been dated by historians to be roughly 2,000 years old and have served to confirm the incredible accuracy of the transmission of the Old Testament by the Jewish scribes. A handwritten copy of every one of the thirty-nine books of the Old Testament were hidden in the Qumran caves (which is beside the Dead Sea) with the exception of the book of Esther. When scholars compared these two-thousand-year-old biblical texts against the oldest biblical manuscripts available, there were no significant textural changes in any of the books.

The Jewish Masoretic scholars had carefully preserved the accuracy of the biblical text to such a remarkable degree that when the scholars examined the Torah, from Genesis to Deuteronomy, there were only 169 Hebrew letters that differed in the Dead Sea Scrolls text from the biblical texts that were used by The King James Bible translators in 1611, which is a widely used version among Christians today.

Significantly, none of the 169 letter variations changed the meaning of a single word. In other words, 99.94% of the letters of the Torah were identical with the texts that had been copied over the centuries. Then in 1979 the Ketef Hinnom Scrolls were discovered and over the next ten years deciphered and published. They also confirm the accurate transcription of the Bible and predate the Dead Sea Scrolls by more than 400 years!

THE EIN-GEDI SCROLL

Finally, the Ein-Gedi Scroll discovered in 1970 was so badly charred and fragile it has been untouched for almost 50 years. Finally it was able to be deciphered by an X-ray imaging technique called microcomputed tomography and contains text from the book of Leviticus, one of the first Old Testament books ever written. It corresponds almost word for word to the many English translations that we now have. We can be confident, therefore, that the Bible has been very meticulously translated for centuries.

AUTHENTICITY

There is powerful evidence that the Old and New Testament documents are based on historical fact and not just a compilation of fables and legends. Some criteria historians use to determine the authenticity and accuracy of ancient texts include how early the sources are to the events they write about, the amount of eye witness testimony, corroborating events, affirmation even from the opposition, and whether or not there are honest yet embarrassing details included in the written testimony. Documents that meet many or all of these criteria are considered trustworthy. In addition, we find detailed promises of a coming Messiah in the very Scripture (Old Testament) that the enemies of the early Christians (Jews) revered as God's Holy Word which were fulfilled in Christ's life. Many of the original Jewish combatants of Jesus and the apostles after comparing these same Scriptures with their fulfillment became Christians because they believed the apostles' testimony and some of these were Jewish leaders and eyewitnesses of Christ themselves. The writers of the New Testament documents wrote about the events within 15-40 years of Jesus' death. The apostle John testified in his Gospel that they (he and the others) heard, saw, and touched Jesus, witnessing many miracles (so many they couldn't all be recorded) and even ate with Jesus after the resurrection.

Titus Flavius Josephus, a non-Christian and the greatest historian of his time wrote about Christ. There is also abundant archeological evidence confirming historical people and places during Jesus' time. Embarrassing details are also among the events the Gospel writers included. For example that the apostles were uneducated, cowardly (hid during the trial and afterward in the upper room), faithless, doubters (Thomas), lied on occasion (Peter), and were not eloquent speakers (Acts). They also record the fact that women were the ones who were the first to witness the empty tomb. A woman's testimony carried no weight in a courtroom in the first century, so if the Gospel writers were trying to convince someone at that time that what they were saying was true, why would they include those details when it could totally discredit their story? Perhaps they were recording those details because it was the truth. The combatant Jews themselves admit the tomb was empty because they concocted a story that the Romans were paid off for stealing Jesus' body. This was widely circulated at that time (see Matthew 28:11-15). There have been many such attempts to discredit the fact of the resurrection and most serious historical scholars today discount all of them. Finally, Saul of Tarsus (later named Paul) was a highly educated, fierce, and zealous Jew and enemy of the early Christians. He publicly approved of their imprisonment, torture, and even murder before his dramatic conversion. His familiarity with the Jewish Scriptures led to his belief that Christ was indeed the Messiah and he went on to author at least thirteen letters of the New Testament.

Some skeptics claim that the Bible is full of contradictions. One example are the claims that because each Gospel contains differing details of certain events that they must not be true. The events are recorded by different people from their own individual perspective. Just because the witnesses never describe what they saw in exactly the same words does not mean they aren't true. It would be suspect indeed if they did and it strengthens the case that they are credible accounts. If they had been colluding a lie, they certainly would have gotten their "stories straight" before recording different versions of each. Finally, the New Testament writers suffered persecution and death for what they believed to be true. Martyrs are certainly sincere for their cause but the New Testament writers were more than just sincere, they were *eyewitnesses* of both miracles and the resurrected Christ. I believe the many criteria used by historians to determine the authenticity of the Bible has convincingly been met.

3

Messianic Prophecy Fulfilled

Perhaps the most convincing evidence of all, that the Bible is truly God-inspired, are the number of fulfilled prophecies found in its pages. Prophecies are declarations by God to His prophets of things that He would accomplish in the future. These included leaders He would raise to power, civilizations, places, events, wars, and kingdoms that would rule. Only God could know all past, present, and future kings and events because He is sovereign and controls all that comes to pass. When we read Daniel 2 for example, he writes about future kingdoms, the rise and fall of the Babylonian, Medeo-Persian, Greek, and Roman empires which reached hundreds of years into the future and happened exactly as he had written. The prophet Isaiah even names Cyrus, 150 years before the future King of Persia is born, and would release the Jews from their exile in Babylon after 70 years of captivity allowing them to return to Jerusalem to rebuild their temple.

Imagine a 16th century man trying to predict inventions like electricity, telephones, cell phones, phonographs, televisions, automobiles, self-driving cars, robots, airplanes, computers, and spacecraft. It would be absolutely impossible for one living in a time of horses and chariots to foresee the amazing technological advances of the last centuries. Yet God can and did.

The foretelling of events in Scripture is irrefutable because we have the paper upon which these prophecies have been written and they have been dated to at least 400 B.C. by the best historical analysts in the world!

God also promised a King who would come one day, die to save His people, judge the world, and rule forever. His title is Messiah, or The Christ and Christians believe that person is Jesus. What we will examine next are just a small sampling of the hundreds of prophecies which concerned the coming of this Messiah. They are sometimes referred to as the Messianic Prophecies and are God's prophets writing about the future King. It is incredible that men who lived *hundreds* of years before Christ wrote things about Him in such specific detail like where He would be born, where He would preach, the miracles He would perform, how He would be killed, and others.

The table below will list the prophecy first, followed by it's Old Testament (OT) reference and then it's fulfillment as recorded in the New Testament (NT) which was written by eyewitnesses of the events. I would encourage anyone desiring verification to look up the references which can be accomplished with any Christian Bible. The Old Testament prediction can also be found in any Hebrew Bible. Keep in mind, the Old Testament was written between approximately 1500-400 B.C. and the New Testament after Jesus ascended in 33 A.D.

Satan will bruise His heel, He would crush his head	Gen 3:15	Heb 2:14, Gal 4:4
Whole world blessed through Abraham's seed	Gen 22:8	Gal 3:8,16
Prophet	Deut 18:15, 18	Acts 3:22, 7:37
Priest	Psa 110:4, Zec 6:13	Heb 5:6, 7:21
King	Isa 9:7, Dan 7:13-14, Zec 6:13	Mt 25:31, Heb 1:8, Lk 1:31,32
Cursed on a tree	Deut 21:23	Gal 3:13
Worshipped by all	Dan 7:14	Mt 2:2, Heb 1:6, Rev 5:8,14, 22:3
Established the New Covenant	Is 42:6, 49:8, Jer 31:31, 32:40 Ez 36:26	Lk 22:20, Heb 8:8-12, 10:16
Lord's anointed	Is 61:1, Psa 2:2 45:7	Lk 4:17
Anointed by God's Spirit	Is 42:1	Mt 3:16
God's delight	Is 42:1	Mt 3:17
Shepherd	Ps 23:1, Is 40:11, Zec 13:7, Ezek 4:23, Mic 5:4	Jn 10:11
Redeemer	Job 19:25-27	Gal 4:4-5, Tit 2:13-14
The Lord's Suffering Servant	Is 53:11	Mt 27:31, Mk 10:45, Jn 6:38
From the tribe of Judah	Gen 49:10, Is 11:1, Mic 5:2	Mt 1:2, Heb 7:14, Rev 5:5

A star would announce His birth	Num 24:17	Mt 2:2
Born of a virgin	Is 7:14	Lk 1:26-27
Born in Bethlehem	Mic 5:2	Mt 2:1
Be called Immanuel (God with us)	Is 7:14, 8:8b, 9:6-7	Mt 1:23
Herod would kill the children	Jer 31:15	Mt 2:16
Escape to Egypt	Hos 11:1	Mt 2:13
Preceded by a messenger	Is 40:3 Mal 3:1	Mt 3:1-3
Elijah would precede Him	Mal 3:1, 4:5-6	Mt 11:13-14
Lamb of God	Ex 12:13, Is 53:7	Jn 1:29,36, Rev 5:8, 12-13, 15:3, 17:14, 19:7,9, 21:14, 21:22
Preach in Galilee	Is 9:1-2	Mt 4:12-17, Lk 23:5
Light for the Gentiles	Is 42:6b	Lk 2:32
Perform miracles	Is 35:5-6	Mt 9:25
Deaf hear, blind see, healer	Is 29:18-19, 42:7, Mal 4:2	Mt 11:5, Jn 9:7
Teach in parables	Ps 78:2 Is 6:9-10	Mt 13:34-35
Chief cornerstone	Ps 118:22-23, Is 28:16	Mt 21:42, Mk 12:10-11, Lk 20:17, Act 4:11, Eph 2:20, 1Pet 2:4-7
Rock of offense	Is 8:14	Rom 9:33, 1Pet 2:8
God's Son	Ps 2:7,12, 89:26	Lk 3:18, 22:70, Jn 1:34, Rom 1:3-4

Falsely accused	Ps 27:12	Mt 26:60, Jn 19:15, Act 2:23, 6:13
Betrayed by a friend	Ps 41:9	Jn 13:18-19, 21
…for 30 pieces of silver	Zec 11:12	Mt 26:14-16
Abandoned by His friends	Zec 13:7	Mt 26:31, Mk 14:27, Lk 23:49
Scorned and wounded	Is 53:7	Mt 27:26
Spit upon	Is 50:6	Mt 26:6-7
Hands and feet pierced	Ps 22:16	Lk 23:33
Killed beside criminals	Is 53:12	Mt 27:38
Lots cast for his clothing	Ps 22:18	Jn 19:23-24
Offered vinegar to drink	Ps 69:21	Mt 27:34
Uttered a forsaken cry	Ps 22:1	Mt 27:46
No bones of His were broken	Ps 34:20	Jn 19:33
Pierced in His side	Zec 12:10	Jn 19:34
Commits His spirit	Ps 31:5	Lk 23:46
Sun would darken	Amos 8:9	Mt 27:45
Buried in a rich man's tomb	Is 53:9	Mt 27:57-60
Would rise from the dead	Ps 16:10	Mk 16:6
3rd day arise	Hos 6:2, Jonah 17:1b	Mt 12:40, Mk 10:34 Jn 2:19
Would ascend to Heaven	Ps 68:18	Act 1:9
Seated at God's right hand	Ps 110:1	Heb 1:3
Called a King	Is 9:7	Jn 18:37
Is the Son of God	Ps 2:7	Mt 3:17

It is remarkable that so many details of the life and death of Jesus could have been fulfilled so perfectly when they were predicted and written down long before He came. It also seems incredible that many of the Jewish religious leaders, who supposedly knew the Old Testament well, could not see this connection even though Jesus told them that Moses and the prophets wrote about Him, (John 5:46, Luke 24:44, 24:27). Sometimes people see only what they want to see (Isaiah 6:10).

The Jews had convinced themselves that their Messiah would be a mighty king and ruler of this world. They had been persecuted for so long and oppressed by the Roman Empire, that they thought their Messiah would come to physically wipe out their oppressors and rule the earth. What happened, God's plan, was not at all what they had expected. Instead of a mighty warrior they got a "Prince of Peace" who rode into their city on a donkey. This just couldn't be the predicted Messiah they had dreamed of! And so, despite all of the incredible miracles that He performed, even to the point of raising Himself and others from the dead, they absolutely refused to believe. Jesus was trying to show them that the kingdom He spoke of is far better than the one they had imagined. While Satan is currently the prince of this world, Jesus is the King of Heaven where He reigns until He comes again (Matthew 4:17).

The following is a quote from the Old Testament describing the coming Messiah that was written hundreds of years before Christ was born. See for yourself how accurately His life was portrayed; yet, the Jews still refused to believe.

> Who has believed our message and to whom has the arm of the LORD been revealed? He grew up before him like a tender shoot, and like a root out of dry ground. He had no beauty or majesty to attract us to him, nothing in his appearance that we should desire him. He was despised and rejected by men, a man of sorrows, and familiar with suffering. Like one from whom men hide their faces he was despised, and we esteemed him not. Surely he took up our infirmities and carried our sorrows, yet we considered him stricken by God, smitten by him, and afflicted.
>
> But he was pierced for our transgressions, he was crushed for our iniquities; the punishment that brought us peace was upon him, and by his wounds we are healed. We all, like sheep, have gone astray, each of us has turned to his own way; and the LORD has laid on him the iniquity of us all. He was oppressed and afflicted, yet he did not open his mouth; he was led like a lamb to the slaughter, and as a sheep before her shearers is silent, so he did not open his mouth. By oppression and judgment he was taken away. And who can speak of his descendants? For he was cut off from the land of the living; for the transgression of my people he was stricken.

> He was assigned a grave with the wicked, and with the rich in his death, though he had done no violence, nor was any deceit in his mouth.
>
> Yet it was the Lord's will to crush him and cause him to suffer, and though the LORD makes his life a guilt offering, he will see his offspring and prolong his days, and the will of the LORD will prosper in his hand. After the suffering of his soul, he will see the light of life and be satisfied; by his knowledge my righteous servant will justify many, and he will bear their iniquities. Therefore I will give him a portion among the great, and he will divide the spoils with the strong, because he poured out his life unto death, and was numbered with the transgressors. For he bore the sin of many, and made intercession for the transgressors (Isaiah 53).

The following passage declares the miracles he would perform when He made the blind see, healed the sick, and cured the deaf. "The eyes of the blind will be opened and the ears of the deaf unstopped. Then the lame will leap like a deer, and the mute tongue shout for joy" (Isaiah 35:5).

These biblical prophecies which came to fruition in every single detail are surely some of the strongest evidences for the truthful claims of Christianity. The eye witness testimony of Christ's many miracles and the resurrection were the final, tangible proofs.

4

Jesus' Identity

Who did Jesus actually claim to be and where had He come from? Many people say that Jesus never claimed to be God but we will see that not only did he claim to be God, He also claimed to be the Messiah (the Christ), the Son of Man, and the Son of God. He also said that He came from being seated at the Father's side in Heaven to make known to man what God is truly like. Not only did Jesus claim these things but He accepted worship on several occasions (an act reserved for God alone), said if we prayed in His name that He would answer (which only God can do), and that He will come with His angels in power and great glory and sit on God's very throne, while God says He shares his glory with no one. Jesus also boldly ascribed the very same names to Himself that God uses for Himself in the Scriptures such as Shepherd, King, Bridegroom, Judge, and many more. Jesus also called others His children, assuming the role of a Father. His followers also claimed His deity (God in the flesh), in the New Testament writings and it is the belief in the deity of Christ that separates Christianity from all other world religions.

Jesus claimed to be:

GOD / The "I AM"

"Anyone who has seen me has seen the Father... I am in the Father, ...and the Father is in me...The words I say to you are not just my own. Rather, it is the Father, living in me, who is doing his work. Believe me when I say that I am in the Father and the Father is in me; or at least believe on the evidence of the miracles themselves" (John 14:9-11).

Thomas said to Jesus, "'My Lord, and my God!' Jesus said to him, 'Have you believed because you have seen me? Blessed are those who have not seen and yet have believed'" (John 20:28-29 ESV).

God said to Moses,
"Say this to the people of Israel: '**I AM** has sent me to you.'...This is my name forever'" (Exodus 3:14).

Jesus said, "Before Abraham was born, **I AM**" (John 8:58) and the Jews tried to stone him to death because they knew exactly what Jesus was saying.

"In my Father's house are many rooms; if it were not so, I would have told you. I am going there to prepare a place for you. And if I go and prepare a place for you, I will come back and take you to be with me that you also may be where **I am**" (John 14:1 ESV).

"**I am** the light of the world," (John 8:12). "**I am** the bread of life" (John 6:35).

"**I am** the gate; whoever enters through **me** will be saved" (John 10:9).

"**I am** the good shepherd. The good shepherd lays down his life for the sheep" (John 10:11).

"**I am** the resurrection and the life. He who believes in **me** will live, even though he dies" (John 11:25).

"**I am** the vine; you are the branches. If you remain in me and I in you, you will bear much fruit; apart from me you can do nothing" (John 15:5).

"**I am** the way and the truth and the life" (John 14:6).

***The Messiah / Christ / Son of Man / Son of God*:**
The Son of Man is the Messiah predicted in the Old Testament, the One who was to come, Israel's King, the

Son of David who would rescue Israel from oppression and suffering and rule the nations from His throne. The Jews were expecting an earthly king who would save them from the oppression of the Romans but Jesus revealed that He was the One who was the King of Heaven who would save them from the oppression and bondage of sin and give them eternal life. Jesus claimed to be that King.

During Jesus' first recorded sermon in the synagogue of Nazareth where He grew up, He read from the scroll of Isaiah (61:1-2) about the Messiah who was to come, and said, "'The Spirit of the Lord is upon **me**, because he has anointed **me** to proclaim good news to the poor. He has sent **me** to proclaim liberty to the captives and recovering of sight to the blind, to set at liberty those who are oppressed, to proclaim the year of the Lord's favor.' And he rolled up the scroll and gave it back to the attendant and sat down. And the eyes of all in the synagogue were fixed on him. And he began to say to them, '**Today** this Scripture has been fulfilled in your hearing'" (Luke 4:17-21 ESV).

When John the Baptist had been imprisoned he sent some of his disciples to ask Jesus, "Are you the one who is to come [the Messiah] or shall we look for another?" And Jesus answered them, "Go and tell John what you hear and see: [a fulfillment of Old Testament prophesies in Isaiah 6] the blind receive their sight and the lame walk, lepers are cleansed and the deaf hear, and the dead are raised up, and the poor have good news preached to them. And blessed is the one who is not offended by me" (Matthew 11:2-6 ESV).

"Unless you believe that **I am He**, you will die in your sins" (John 8:24 ESV).

"I saw in the night visions, and behold, with the clouds of heaven there came one like a **son of man**, and he came to the Ancient of Days and was presented before him. And to him was given **dominion** and **glory** and a **kingdom**, that all peoples, nations, and languages should serve him; his dominion is an everlasting dominion, which shall not pass away, and **his kingdom** one that **shall not be destroyed**" (Daniel 7:13-14 ESV).

Referencing the above passage, Jesus claimed He was that Son of Man (the Son of God) and a King. He said,

"When the **Son of Man** comes in his glory, and all the angels with him, **he will sit on his throne** in heavenly **glory**. All the nations will be gathered before him, and he will separate the people one from another as a shepherd separates the sheep from the goats" (Matthew 25:31 ESV).

"Truly, truly, I say to you, whoever hears my word and believes him who sent me has eternal life. He does not come into judgment, but has passed from death to life. Truly, truly, I say to you, an hour is coming, and is now here, when the dead will hear the voice of the **Son of God**, and those who hear will live. For as the Father has life in himself, so he has granted the Son also to have life in himself. And he has given him authority to execute judgment, because **he is the Son of Man**" (John 5:24-27 ESV).

After healing a blind man Jesus asked him, "Do you believe in **the Son of Man**?" He answered, "And who is he, sir, that I may believe in him?" Jesus said to him, "You have seen him, and **it is he who is speaking to you**." He said, "Lord, I believe," and **he worshiped him**" (John 9:35-37 ESV).

Jesus asked the disciples, "'Who do you say that I am?'" Simon Peter replied, 'You are the **Christ**, the **Son** of the living **God**.' And Jesus answered him, 'Blessed are you, Simon Bar-Jonah! For flesh and blood has not revealed this to you, but my Father who is in heaven'" (Matthew 16:15-17 ESV).

"Then he strictly charged the disciples to tell no one that **he was the Christ**" (Matthew 16:20 ESV).

The woman from Samaria at the well said, "'I know that **Messiah** (called Christ) is coming. When he comes, he will explain everything to us.' Then Jesus declared, 'I, the one speaking to you—**I am he**'" (John 4:25-26 ESV).

Then when she told the people in her community about Jesus they investigated themselves and professed, "We know that this man really is the **Savior** of the world" (John 4:42).

After Lazarus had been dead for four days and Jesus brought him back to life, He said to Martha,

"**I am** the resurrection and the life. The one who believes in **me** will live, even though they die; and whoever lives by believing in **me** will never die. Do you believe this?" "Yes, Lord," she replied, "I believe that you are the **Messiah**, the **Son of God**, who is to come into the world" (John 11:25-27).

Jesus did not correct her. It is absolutely clear that Jesus claimed to be the coming Messiah.

He also claims that he is the ONLY way to God:

> "No one comes to the Father except through me" (John 14:6).
>
> "Heaven and earth will pass away, but my words will never pass away" (Matthew 24:35).
>
> One cannot believe in God without believing in His Son:
>
> "He who hates me hates my Father as well" (John 15:23).

The writers of the New Testament who knew Jesus in the flesh also claimed He was God:

> John writes, "In the beginning was the Word, and the **Word was with God**, and **the Word was God**. He was in the beginning with God. **All things were made through him**, and without him was not any thing made that was made" (John 1:1-3 ESV). He says Jesus was the Creator of all things.
>
> Paul, writes, "Christ, who **is the image of God**" (2 Corinthians 4:4). "Christ Jesus, … was **in the form of God**…" (Philippians 2:6 ESV).
>
> "He **is the image of the invisible God**,… **by him all things were created**… in him all the fullness of God was pleased to dwell" (Colossians 1:15, 19 ESV).
>
> "In him the whole fullness of **deity** dwells bodily" (Colossians 2:9 ESV).
>
> "To the King of the ages, immortal, invisible, **the only God**, be honor and glory forever and ever" (1 Timothy 1:17 ESV).
>
> "**There is one God**, and there is one mediator between God and men, **the man Christ Jesus**" (1 Timothy 2:5 ESV).

"Our Lord Jesus Christ… is the blessed and only **Sovereign**, the King of kings and Lord of lords" (1 Timothy 6:14,15 ESV).

"Our great **God** and Savior **Jesus Christ**," (Titus 2:13).

"**God** our Savior **appeared**, he saved us," (Titus 3:4,5) "The **Christ**, who **is God** over all" (Romans 9:5b ESV)

The author of Hebrews wrote, "His Son, whom he appointed the heir of all things, through whom also **he created the world**. He is the radiance of the glory of God and the **exact imprint of his nature**" (Hebrews 1:2,3 ESV).

The Apostle Peter wrote, "Our **God** and Savior **Jesus Christ**" (2Peter 1:1).

John the Apostle wrote, "**Jesus Christ**. He **is** the true **God** and eternal life" (1 John 5:20).

"No one has ever seen God, but the one and only **Son**, who **is** himself **God**…(John 1:18)

In summary, Jesus claimed to be God, Messiah (the Christ), and the only way to be saved. His followers declared the same message and Paul proclaimed, "If you confess with your mouth that Jesus is Lord and believe in your heart that God raised him from the dead, you will be saved" (Romans 10:9 ESV).

Jesus also claimed names and roles for Himself that are reserved for God alone and that He was not simply a man but came from Heaven (having always been at the Father's side):

> "I came from God... He sent me" (John 8:42 ESV).
>
> To do the Father's will which was to give everlasting life to all whom God gave to the Son (John 6:33-51).

He received worship on nine occasions when only God deserves worship:

> (Exodus 34:14, 1 Chronicles 16:29, Matthew 8:2, 9:18, 14:33, 15:25, 20:20, 28:17, Mark 5:6, John 9:38, 20:28).
>
> He forgives sins: (2 Chronicles 7:14, Jeremiah 31:34, Matthew 9:2).
>
> Answers prayers: (Job 22:27, Jeremiah 29:12, John 14:13-14).
>
> Is a King: (Isaiah 44:6, John 18:36-37)

Savior: (2Samuel 22:3, Psalm 17:7, 106:21, Isaiah 43:3, 43:11, Hosea 13:4, Matthew 1:21, Luke 2:11, 19:10).

Shepherd: (Psalm 23:1, Isaiah 40:11, Ezekiel 34:15, Zechariah 10:2-3, Matthew 25:32-33, John 10:11).

Light: (Isaiah 42:6, Psalm 4:6, 27:1, John 8:12, 9:5).

Rock: (Deuteronomy 32:4, 32:15, 2 Samuel 22:3, Isaiah 44:8, Habakkuk 1:12, 1 Corinthians 10:4).

Bridegroom: (Isaiah 62:5, Matthew 9:15).

Gives life: (Genesis 2:7, Job 33:4, Deuteronomy 32:39, John 3:15-16, Mark 5:41, Luke 7:14, John 11:43-44).

In the role of a father: (Psalm 34:11, 149:2, Isaiah 63:8, 1Kings 6:13, Joel 2:23, "my son" Matthew 9:2b, "daughter" 9:22, "my children" Mark 10:24, "little children'" John 21:5.

Receives glory: (Isaiah 42:8, Matthew 25:31, John 17:5).

The Judge: (Joel 3:12, Psalm 82:7, Matthew 25:31, John 5:22, 27).

Holy One: (Isaiah 43:3, 5:19, Ezekiel 39:7, Mark 1:24, Luke 4:34, John 6:69, Revelation 3:7).

Lord: (Exodus 6:7, Ezekiel 11:12, Matthew 7:22, 25:31-46).

Seated on God's throne: (1 Kings 22:19, Isaiah 6:1, Psalm 11:4, Matthew 25:31-46).

The Almighty: (Genesis 35:11, Revelation 1:8).

First and Last (Alpha/Omega): (Isaiah 41:4, 44:6, Revelation 1:8, 17, 21:6).

No wonder the Jews were incensed and sought to kill him. Either Jesus was out of His mind *or* He was exactly who He claimed to be.

Jesus undeniably claimed to be God and the evidences that Christ used to prove that He was supernaturally sent from God are many. First, He is the only man who ever lived a perfect and sinless life. Of the hundreds of historians who have written about Christ, Christians and non-Christians alike, not one of them ever dared to accuse him of sin with one exception: the Jewish leaders who heard Him claim equal standing with God (which indeed He had) and they called it "blasphemy." He was not a man born with original sin; He was God.

Other evidence includes His many well-documented miracles and, his ultimate resurrection from the dead.

He changed water to wine, healed scores of sick people, restored sight to the blind, drove out demons, created food to feed thousands, walked on water, calmed a raging storm, and even raised the dead to life. The list is endless.

John wrote, "Now Jesus did many other signs in the presence of the disciples, which are not written in this book; but these are written so that you may believe that Jesus is the Christ, the Son of God, and that by believing you may have life in his name" (John 20:30-31 ESV).

The single most critical question a person can ask himself during his lifetime is, "Who do I believe Jesus to be?" The two most common opinions about Jesus' identity are that He was truly the Son of God, or that He was simply a good person and nothing more. He could not possibly be both. Jesus told the disciples that many of them would suffer terrible persecution because of Him and that many would die as the direct result of proclaiming His name faithfully to the world. It is believed that all of the apostles, with the exception of John, were murdered for their belief in Christ and that none of them denied Him even when faced with death. We have seen that these men were eyewitnesses to Jesus' miracles, His sinless life, His crucifixion, and most importantly, His resurrection. They were totally convinced of His identity and that He was exactly who He claimed to be. If it were untrue, would they all die for what they knew was a lie?

Since the resurrection, millions of Christian martyrs have been true to Jesus to the very end despite severe persecution. Many were stoned to death, some were roasted slowly over a fire until dead (see Foxe's Book of Martyrs), some were crucified, cannibalized, and others viciously tortured. It is reported that over 100,000 Christians are violently killed annually because of their faith. Would all these people also die for a lie?

It is worth noting that Christians are persecuted and are willing to die witnessing for Jesus Christ and the truth He proclaimed. Jesus said, "You will be my witnesses… to the ends of the earth" (Acts 1:8). "Whoever loses his life for my sake will find it" (Matthew 10:39). He also said some of them would be beaten, imprisoned, put to death, and hated for His name's sake (Matthew 10:17,21,22, Revelation 2:10a.) But to "be faithful unto death and I will give you the crown of life" (Revelation 2:10b).

The distinction between Christian martyrs and those of other faiths is that the Christians are *being* killed for their faith in a *person*, while the others *are* killing for their religious *cause*.

Either Jesus was exactly who He claimed to be or He was an evil and cruel deceiver. If He were not, in fact, the true Son of God and all He spoke was not true then He was the cause of all sorts of wicked atrocities and could not ever be considered a 'good' man. A good man would never let innocent people die for his lies. In addition, He could not have performed all of those miracles if He were simply a man.

Many people, Christians or not, believe He was gentle, loving, warm, and wonderful. Since He could not have been just a good person, as some believe, then He was either a liar, a lunatic, or God's Son.

The famous writer, C.S. Lewis, said,

> A man who was merely a man and said the sort of things Jesus said would not be a great moral teacher. He would either be a lunatic—on the level of a man who says he is a poached egg—or else he would be the devil of hell. You must take your choice. Either this was, and is, the Son of God; or else a madman or something worse. You can shut Him up for a fool... or you can fall at His feet and call Him Lord and God. But let us not come up with any patronizing nonsense about His being a great human teacher. He has not left that open to us, nor did He intend to, (*Mere Christianity*).

There is no way a person can simply ignore the question, "Who do I believe Jesus to be?" It is the most important determination a person can make. Is it really worth the eternal consequences to run from the question and pretend it can remain unanswered? Or is it more sensible to conclude that it must be addressed and answered to the best of our ability? The only way to be truthful to ourselves is to confront this situation head-on and weigh the evidence before us. Jesus leaves no middle ground on which to hide. He says there are only two sides and we must choose which one we are on.

Christ provided evidence that He was sent from God by His many miracles which were witnessed by thousands, as the Gospels record. One very convincing one was when Jesus raised Lazarus from the grave. A great crowd was present for the event, including the leaders opposed to Jesus, and the man had been dead for four days! Jesus simply called out, "Lazarus, come forth!" The man in the tomb, wrapped in burial linens, simply rose up and walked toward the onlookers. Here Jesus demonstrated that He truly does have power over life and death. And that is when the religious leaders commenced a most intensive plot to kill him.

If a person elects not to believe that Jesus was sent by God, what evidence is he basing this crucial assumption on? It is tempting to base our beliefs on past experiences instead of the facts. Many people have decided the issue as a result of what others have said or done. Many of us have observed the hypocritical and self-righteous behaviors of some who've claimed to be Christians and on that basis, have decided not to have any part of it. Sadly, there are some people who may have faith but fail to reflect it in their lives which presents a weak testimony for the sake of others who may want to know more about Christianity. There are others who have a great deal of faith but they become so passionate about what they know to be true, they can turn others away with their unintentional aggressiveness.

The Bible teaches Christians, "Always be prepared to give an answer to everyone who asks you to give the reason for the hope that you have. But do this with gentleness and respect" (1 Peter 3:15).

God wants us to share why we believe with nonbelievers and the reasons for the hope that we have, but He has instructed that this be done with humility and respect for others. However, some become so concerned with who will make it to heaven that they can become condemning and judgmental. Fortunately, it is not our job to make that determination and we should be careful not to judge another's level of faith. Regardless of our past experiences observing other fallible, although well-intentioned Christians, we can rely on the truth about who Jesus was based on the well-documented facts of His life.

Therefore, if what Peter said was true and that, "There is salvation in no one else, for there is no other name under heaven given among men by which we must be saved" (Acts 4:12 ESV) then the next question one might ask is, "What about other religions? Is Jesus truly the only way to God, and eternal life in Heaven?"

OTHER RELIGIONS

Some people believe that all religions worship the same God and that there are many ways to get to heaven. In addition, most other world religions base blessings and salvation on what a person does or how good they were during their life. The crucial difference between all religions and Christianity is that Christians believe that God is three Persons in one essence: The Father, the Son, and the Holy

Spirit. This is called the Trinity. One simple way to try and explain this deep theological topic, is to say that God is the same being, acting in three different roles, to accomplish His purposes. God the Father plans , God the Son executes the plan, and God the Holy Spirit applies the plan to our lives. There are a few passages in the Old Testament that show the Three communicating with each other:

"Let **us** make man in **our** image, after **our** likeness" (Genesis 1:26 NIV). "Behold, the man has become like one of **us**" (3:22 ESV), "Come, let **us** go down and there confuse their language" (11:7 ESV) , "Who will go for **us**?" (Is 6.8), "Who has believed what he has heard from **us**?" (53.1), "'Awake, O sword, against my shepherd, against the **man who stands next to me,**' declares the Lord of hosts" (Zechariah 13:7 ESV).

I believe there is plenty of scriptural evidence for the doctrine of the Trinity but those of other faiths do not. They may revere and honor Jesus as a great prophet or teacher and even may claim that they are saved by His sacrifice but they do not accept His claims to be God in the flesh. Jews reject His claim that He is their long awaited Messiah, Muslims deny He is God's Son, and Mormons and Jehovah's Witnesses say He was created and there is no Trinity, Buddhists and Hindus believe He was an enlightened teacher, and most of these disbelieve the resurrection. As for the Spirit, others do not agree that He is a person, yet the Spirit in scripture grieves, convicts, counsels, guides and communicates among other things. So that is the greatest distinction between Christians and others.

Then we have the doctrine of grace which is the belief that salvation if a free gift that comes through faith in the sinless life of Christ. Many religions believe they can earn God's favor all on their own contrary to what has been written in the Bible. Some believe parts of the Bible and many claim it has been misinterpreted or corrupted over time and that other books have been added as authoritative scripture. Some examples include the Jewish Talmud, the Islamic Quran and Hadith, the Mormon's Book of Mormon, the Jehovah's Witnesses New World Translation, the Hindu's Bhagwat Gita, and the Buddhist's Tipitaka.

Christians believe the Bible contains no errors whatsoever and that it has been accurately translated and preserved through time and Christianity is the ONLY religion that bases blessing and salvation *solely* on belief in Jesus and the good He has done on the believer's behalf which includes His sinless life, death, resurrection, and ascension.

The Bible says that no one is saved by good deeds of his own: "By grace you have been saved through faith, and not of yourselves; it is the gift of God, not of works, lest anyone should boast" (Ephesians 2:8-9).

"But when the kindness of God our Savior and His love for mankind appeared, He saved us, not on the basis of deeds which we have done in righteousness, but according to His mercy, by the washing of regeneration and renewing by the Holy Spirit, whom He poured out upon us richly through Jesus Christ our Savior, that being justified by His grace we might be made heirs according to the hope of eternal life" (Titus 3:4-7).

It is a very sad situation that many churches and religions teach that we are saved by our good deeds on Earth which is blatantly contrary to what Jesus taught. I would caution anyone who is misled by these claims which are made by many various churches and other religions. God is very specific in His Word that there is nothing we can do ourselves to deserve salvation or earn it. The true Christian Church is the one that teaches the Bible and only the Bible as the final authority on any spiritual matter. Though men have led many astray, God has preserved the Bible all these years as the one and only true source of knowledge of Him and His plan of salvation. Some people in the past have wanted to alter this plan by either adding to or subtracting from the Bible. God knew this would happen and warned in the final chapter of His Book:

"If anyone adds to these things, God will add to him the plagues that are written in this book; and if anyone takes away from the words of the book of this prophecy, God shall take away his part from the Book of Life" (Revelation 22:19 NKJV).

Here we will examine just two examples of religious groups that have added to God's words: Mormons and Muslims. Mormons believe that membership in the Church of Latter-Day Saints is the only way to heaven:

> "**If it had not been for Joseph Smith** and the restoration, there would be no salvation outside the Church of Jesus Christ of Latter-Day Saints."[24]

> "We believe the Bible to be the Word of God **in so far as it is translated correctly**. . . . We **also** believe the Book of Mormon to be the Word of God."[25]

> "Believe in God, believe in Jesus, **and** believe in Joseph his prophet, **and** Brigham his successor and,... you shall be saved in the kingdom of God... No man or woman will ever enter into the Celestial kingdom of God without **the consent of Joseph Smith**... every man and woman **must** have the certificate of Joseph Smith, Jr. as a passport to their entrance into the mansions where God and Christ are..."[26]

I find it rather presumptuous that a man born in 1801 would claim to have received the only 'true' revelation regarding God's Word and Jesus' life while we have eye witness, written accounts in the Gospels which have been dated to within a few decades of Jesus' lifetime. It is clear that the Mormon founders have added much to God's Word.

Islam is the world's second largest and fastest growing religion. Muslims believe that Muhammed was the 'last' great prophet who claimed that his revelations were received directly from God through the 'archangel' Gabriel. He recited and his 'disciples' recorded these revelations in the Quran (sometimes referred to as the Koran) which is the standard by which the Muslims test the Holy Scriptures. They do not believe the New Testament account of Jesus, only the account recorded in the Quran. The Quran adamantly states that Jesus was no more than an Apostle and not God incarnate or God's Son.

> *Sura 4:171 "Oh People of the Book* [Christians]*! Commit no excess in your religion: nor say of Allah anything but the truth. Christ Jesus, son of Mary, was* ***no more than*** *a* ***messenger...of Allah and His Word****...believe in Allah and His messengers.* ***Do not say, 'Trinity'****: desist: it will be better for you: for* ***Allah is one God****: Glory be to Him...* ***far exalted is He above having a son!*** *To Him belong all things in the heavens and the earth."*

The Apostle John said that God created all things through and for Jesus Christ.

> *5:73 "****They do blaspheme who say: God is one of three in a trinity****: for there is no God but except one god (Allah)."*

> *43:59* ***"He*** [Jesus] ***was no more than a servant."***

> *17:111 "Praise be to Allah, Who* ***begets no son*** *and has no partner in (His) dominion."*

> *19:88-92 "They say: 'Allah Most Gracious has begotten a son!' Indeed you have put forth a thing most monstrous!... it is not consonant with the*

majesty of (Allah) Most Gracious that He should beget a ***son****..."; 17:111 "He has no partner in His dominion..."*

18:5 "It is a grievous thing that issues from their mouths...What they say is nothing but falsehood!"

They also don't believe that Jesus actually died on the cross:

4:157 "... ***they did not kill him,*** [Jesus] ***nor crucify him,*** *but so it was made to appear to them and those who differ therein are full of doubts... for a surety they did not kill him-Nay, Allah raised him unto himself."*

They claim Jews and Christians changed the words of the Bible:

3:78 "They distorted the Book..."

2:59 "the transgressors changed the Word that was given them..."

2:75 "A party of them heard the Word of Allah and perverted it knowingly--Woe to those!"

Of course we now know that the words have remained accurate since the discovery of the Dead Sea Scrolls (discussed in an earlier chapter).

Some Muslims claim Islam is a peaceful religion but they also revere their prophet and founder, Muhammed who is said to have inspired the words of the Quran and they are very violent against unbelievers. There is a major contrast between Muhammed and Jesus. The latter insisted on peace and loving even one's enemies while the former commands that his followers fight against unbelievers in the cause of Allah, martyrs, who will earn the highest reward in heaven:

> *3:76 "**Those who believe, fight** in the cause of Allah and those who reject the faith fight in the cause of evil--so **you are fighting friends of Satan...**"*
>
> *4:89 "...**seize them and slay them** wherever you find them..."*
>
> *9:5 "...lay in wait for them in every strategem of **war**..."*
>
> *9:111 "theirs* [in return] *is the Garden* [of Paradise]:"... [for those who] *"fight in His Cause, and slay and are slain... rejoice in the **bargain**..."* [Men do not make bargains with Almighty God.]
>
> *5:51 "Oh, you who believe! **Take not the Jews and Christians for your friends**... they are but friends and protectors to each other. And he amongst*

you that turns to them [for friendship] *is of them. Verily, Allah guides not a people unjust."*

62:6 "O you that stand on Judaism! If you think that you are friends of Allah, to the exclusion of other men, then express your desire for Death, if you are truthful!"

*21:92 "This **brotherhood** of yours is a single Brotherhood... therefore serve me* [Allah] *and no other."*

59:2-4 [The first battle at Mecca where they rejected Muhammad]: *"It is He Who got out the Unbelievers among the People of the Book from their homes at the first gathering (of the forces)* [of Muhammad]... *they thought their fortresses would defend them from Allah! But the **wrath** of Allah... cast **terror** into their hearts, so that they **destroyed** their dwellings by their own hands and the hands of the Believers* [in Allah and Muhammad]... *they shall certainly have the **punishment** of the Fire. That is because they resisted Allah and His Messenger."*

*61:4 "Truly Allah loves those who **fight** in His Cause in battle array."*

*61:10-12 "O you who believe! Shall I lead you to a **bargain** that will save you from a*

> *grievous penalty?- That you believe in Allah and His Messenger, and that you strive your utmost in the Cause of Allah, with your property and your persons...* ***He will forgive your sins****, and admit you to...beautiful mansions in Gardens of Eternity: that is indeed the supreme Achievement."*
>
> *48:16 "...You shall be summoned to* ***fight*** *against a people...if you show obedience, Allah will grant you a goodly reward, but if you turn back... He will punish you with a grievous penalty."*
>
> *9:52 "Can you expect for us any fate other than one of two glorious things - martyrdom or victory?"*
>
> *48:13 "if any do not believe in Allah and His Messenger* [Muhammad], *We have prepared, for the Unbelievers, a Blazing Fire!"*

An article in *USA Today* quoted a commander of the al-Qaeda forces, "We will fight to the last breath for the supremacy of Islam..."

Muslim suicide bombers and soldiers are martyrs whose intent is to kill for their cause: the establishment of Islam as a world religion and government. Christian martyrs, on the other hand, are willing to **be** killed for speaking about and never denying their Lord and Savior, Jesus Christ.

Switching gears, while God defined marriage as being between one man and woman, Muslims are permitted multiple wives:

> *4:3 "...marry women of your choice, two, or three, or four..."*

God said a man shall have one wife and the two shall become one (Genesis 2:24). The man will love, cherish, and take care of his wife just as his own body (Ephesians 5:28).

And while Jesus honored and respected women, Muslims are allowed to mistreat them:

> *4:15-16 "As for those of your women who are guilty of immoral conduct,... confine those women to their houses until either death takes them away or Allah opens some way for them."*

> *4:34 "As to those* ***women*** *on whose part you fear disloyalty and ill-conduct, admonish them first, next, refuse to share their beds, and last* ***beat them...***"

Allah loves only the "righteous" and not the sinner:

> The Qur'an states that Allah does not love sinners or evildoers (Sura 2:190; 3:57, 140; 4:36; 5:64; 28:77; 31:18; 42:40; 57:23). Yet, "God shows

> his love for us in that while we were still sinners, Christ died for us," (Romans 5:8).

Allah is a fierce God full of wrath who commands violence. Muslims say he is merciful yet he calls for murder and bloodshed with rewards for the martyr and the mistreatment of women. He fiercely denies that God has a Son (which is Satan's favorite tactic) since He is the only way for a soul to be saved and escape Satan's grip. The God I speak of and adore is one who calls Himself a servant (Matthew 20:28), and who comes to call not the righteous, but sinners (Matthew 9:13, Mark 2:17, 5:32). He came not to *be* served but *to* serve, save, suffer, and die for the lives of His children (Matthew 16:21, Mark 8:31, 9:12). That is the God whom I serve.

The major problem with accepting Muhammed's testimony is that it occurred 600 years *after* Jesus, while the New Testament contains eyewitness and firsthand testimony of the life and ministry of Christ. In addition, the Old Testament was written from approximately 1400 to 400 BC, and is literally filled with *hundreds* of prophecies that Jesus would come and do precisely what was written of Him. This makes Muhammed's testimony approximately 2,000 years out of date and it greatly lacks credibility since he was a mere man who never performed any miracles himself to prove his 'authority' as a prophet sent from God. His claims of having the truth of the scriptures revealed only to him are based entirely on personal 'visions.'

Jesus warned that prophets would come speaking lies: "False Christs and false prophets will arise...to lead astray, if possible, even the elect. See, I have told you beforehand" (Matthew 24:24-25 ESV).

Paul nails it perfectly:

"Even if we or an angel from heaven should preach to you a gospel contrary to the one we preached to you, let him be accursed" (Galatians 1:8 ESV).

I find it inconceivable that almost two billion people would follow such a person who claimed to have received the *only* accurate interpretation of God's Word. It is preposterous for a 'religion' to claim that they have the only correct interpretation of the Bible which implies that all Christians, including the very students of Jesus who founded the Christian Church, have misinterpreted the Lord's teachings from the start and their 'prophet' was the only person who got it right. Yet, this man has absolutely nothing to back up such a claim in terms of evidence that he was truly sent from God.

Jesus Christ, on the other hand, displayed enormous credibility through His miracles and resurrection. In addition, does it make any sense that God would dispatch Muslim terrorists to set the world straight? The extremist Muslim claims mass murder is authorized in the name of Allah.

The following is a quote from a *Nightline* interview of Osama bin Laden on May 28,1998 and was included in the first printing of this book in 2000:

> He has issued calling on Muslims to kill Americans where they can, regardless of whether they are soldiers or civilians... Allah ordered us in this religion to purify Muslim land of all nonbelievers...We all work for Allah and await his reward.

It is eerie that the attack on America would follow only one year later ushering in the current war on terror. Although God once condoned violence, it was to achieve His specific purposes and to be carried out only by His direction and in a precisely defined manner. God clearly teaches that men are to be condemned for taking justice into their own hands. Often in Old Testament times God specifically instructed the Israelites to go to war to drive out heathen nations whose people were engaged in all sorts of evil practices such as idolatry, witchcraft, sacrificing their children and burning those bodies on altars where they worshipped false gods. One purpose of those judgments was to purge the area of extreme wickedness while His chosen people went through the process of conquering the Promised Land and defining its borders. Keep in mind that the Israelites were not acting on their own, but obeying God's decrees.

These judgments as well as the flood, the destruction of Sodom and Gomorrah, and the plagues of Egypt, are just some examples of how the Lord metes out justice and that not only is He capable of it, but that He has done it and will do it again in the inevitable, inescapable final judgment that He has promised. God has never broken a promise yet and we should heed His warnings very seriously indeed.

God's relationship to His children, as revealed through His Son Jesus, was to be very different and is one reason it was called the 'New' Covenant. In the New Testament Jesus never encourages violence; He always condemns it. The "eye for an eye and tooth for tooth" mentality (which has been totally misunderstood and taken out of context) was clarified by Jesus to forgive and have compassion toward all, even toward one's enemies.

Jesus said, "All who draw the sword will die by the sword" (Matthew 26:52).

"Love your enemies and pray for those who persecute you, that you may be sons of your Father in heaven" (Matthew 5:44).

"If someone strikes you on the right cheek, turn to him the other also. If someone wants to sue you and take your tunic, let him have your cloak as well" (Matthew 5:39,40).

Paul wrote, "Do not take revenge, my friends, but leave room for God's wrath, for it is written: 'It is mine to avenge; I will repay,' says the Lord. On the contrary: If your enemy is hungry, feed him; if he is thirsty, give him something to drink. In doing this, you will heap burning coals on his head. Do not be overcome by evil, but overcome evil with good" (Romans 12:19-21).

Jesus couldn't have said it better, "A time is coming when anyone who kills you will think he is offering a service to God. They will do such things because they have not known the Father or me. I have told you this, so that when the time comes you will remember that I warned you" (John 16:2-4).

It should be obvious to us by now that rarely anything is accomplished through violence. Bloody conflicts continue to rage throughout the world today, yet the same old problems are never solved. Terrorism and wars across the globe are perfect examples of men in conflict who, in a futile attempt, keep trying to solve their issues through violent means. Only One has the authority to execute judgment on men and He will, at His predetermined time.

Jesus warned, "Beware of false prophets, who come to you in sheep's clothing, but inwardly they are ravenous wolves. You will know them by their fruits… every good tree bears good fruit, but a bad tree bears bad fruit… Every tree that does not bear good fruit is cut down and thrown into the fire. Therefore by their fruits you will know them" (Matthew 7:15-20 NKJ).

"Many false prophets have gone out into the world. By this you know the Spirit of God: Every spirit that confesses that Jesus Christ has come in the flesh is of God, and every spirit that does not confess that Jesus Christ has come in the flesh is not of God" (1 John 4:1-3 NKJ).

A person can be totally sincere about his religion, but he can also be sincerely wrong. A 'religious' person has a real problem if he is worshipping the wrong God no matter how sincere he is. For example, a person can believe in a God of his own making. Many people have formulated a God that they've defined in their own minds based on what they think He should be like. Many people who believe in God have never even opened a Bible to learn what He is really like. They give their God attributes in accordance with their individual tastes.

For example, some only want to believe in a God of love who is incapable of anger, wrath, or final judgment. In doing this they basically pick and choose what they like, and thus, create a false God for themselves. Belief in false Gods is severely condemned throughout both Testaments. Moses wrote, "Be careful, or you will be enticed to turn away and worship other gods and bow down to them. Then the Lord's anger will burn against you, and he will shut the heavens so that it will not rain and the ground will yield no produce, and you will soon perish from the good land the LORD is giving you" (Deuteronomy 11:16).

A recent article in *Life* magazine reported that over 95% of the world's population believe in a god. If that is the case, then I wonder why Jesus said, "Enter through the narrow gate. For wide is the gate and broad is the road that leads to destruction, and many enter through it. But small is the gate and narrow the road that leads to life, and only a few find it" (Matthew 7:13).

We must be certain first that there is one true God. Fortunately for us, God has made it easy to determine who He is by sending His Son who is the exact representation of God himself.

5

Original Sin

God commanded Adam: "You must not eat from the tree of the knowledge of good and evil, for when you eat of it you will surely die" (Genesis 2:17).

"'You will not surely die,' the serpent said to the woman. 'For God knows that when you eat of it your eyes will be opened, and you will be like God, knowing good and evil'" (Genesis 3:4-5 ESV).

Notice God was giving the first man and woman a choice to believe and obey Him. He also revealed that the sin of disobedience would result in death. The serpent (Satan) appealed to the man's desire to be like God Himself implying that he had no need for God and that he could be one himself. Satan deceived Adam and Eve into thinking they had a 'right' to do whatever they felt they wanted to do. Therefore, sin is this disposition which is inherited from Adam to do whatever we want and to make ourselves the center around which our whole world revolves. It is the tendency to put ourselves first and our needs above others.

If you don't believe this is a literally inherited attitude we all share, just consider how a newborn baby or toddler acts when his desires are not met immediately. He may even throw a violent temper tantrum until he gets what he wants. It is the natural tendency for a child to lash out in fury when a parent is not paying attention to him or when a sibling takes something of his. It is the reason a toddler abhors discipline. Contrary to what many people believe, it does not appear to be our 'nature' to be 'good' at all! Mustn't this self-centered tendency be unlearned as we teach our children to be polite, respectful, and obedient for their own good?

If one doesn't believe that it is in our 'nature' to sin, I believe I can convince you. Isn't it much harder to do the 'right' thing than the 'wrong' thing? For example, if a grocer were to accidentally give a person $20 more change than was due him, wouldn't he tend to want to keep it? Isn't it much harder to point out the error and give it back? If we think we can get away with something because it will go unnoticed, don't we have to literally fight with our conscience to do the right thing? Doesn't that prove that it is unnatural for us to want to do the morally right thing? Many times we will only decide against a selfish desire to avoid the 'consequences' of an act, not because we would naturally do otherwise but because we might get caught. We may not steal or murder because it could mean arrest; or we may decide against adultery because we would eventually be found out and it would do irreparable damage to our marriage.

We rarely, if ever, do what is morally right because it is natural for us. The laws, which govern society today, had their origin with the commandments that God passed down to us through Moses and the Israelites.

Our judicial system is practically a mirror image of the one God instituted for His people many years ago and can be verified by reviewing the Old Testament. God told the Israelites they were to appoint judges and that a man could not be condemned without the testimony of two or more witnesses. Even today we rely on several witnesses when presenting a case in our courts and in America they are still required to swear on the Bible. This system originated with God and His people thousands of years ago and remains a vital part of a democratic society. God knew that this self-centered behavior would lead to death as Cain proved when he committed the first murder and killed his brother Abel out of jealousy. God commanded Adam to be obedient because God loved him and knew what was best for him and that sin would lead to all kinds of undesirable and immoral behavior. This would lead to man's ultimate unhappiness and self-imposed destruction.

The sin of the human race is the disposition of self-realization and the 'right to myself' attitude. The sinful nature causes harmful emotions within us that manifest themselves through our actions, which often result in hurting another human being. Was God showing love toward us when He commanded us to obey Him? Was it that He knew how badly sin would hurt us? Or was He just telling us what to do? Couldn't God have created us to serve and obey Him for His own enjoyment? Yes, He could have and we would basically be slaves, forced to worship Him. It is precisely because of God's love for us that He allows evil to exist so that we are still left with the freedom to follow Him or not. Knowing that He has let us choose to do evil or good should invoke an even greater love for Him. Christ came to save all mankind; therefore all must be sinners. "There is not a righteous man on earth who does what is right and never sins" (Ecclesiastes 7:20).

"Just as sin entered the world through one man, and death through sin, … in this way death came to all men, because all sinned" (Romans 5:12).

If you have ever lied, stolen, broken a law, wanted something another person has, been unfaithful, angry with another person, or even disobeyed your parents, then you have sinned. God says sin will be judged and that all mankind deserves judgment and that the penalty is death, separated from Him forever. God is both good and just. His justice demands that He punish all wrongs ever committed. If evil were left unpunished, then God could not be considered good. But because God loves man, He provided a solution. Someone who would cover our sin, a sinless Savior who would pay the penalty for us and take our deserved punishment. All one needs to do is accept it; it is a free gift of grace by God's mercy. That Savior is Christ.

The offer of forgiveness requires a response. The response God seeks is recognition of our sinful condition (confessing), repentance (being sorry), turning away (willingness to change), and accepting Christ's offer of salvation (making Him Lord in our lives and trusting

Him to change us). Even though we have all inherited a sin-nature, nowhere in Scripture does God condemn a man for that inheritance, but for refusing to acknowledge God's solution to the problem and His costly gift of salvation by the work of Christ.

Oswald Chambers put it this way,

> The condemnation is not that I am born with a heredity of sin, but if when I realize Jesus Christ came to deliver me from it, I refuse to let Him do so, from that moment I begin to get the seal of damnation. 'And this is the judgment:' (the critical moment), 'that the light is come into the world, and men loved darkness rather than the light'.[22]

What exactly is sin and why do we need a Savior according to God? In considering the question of sin we are faced with two startling facts: one, that man makes so little of sin, and two, that God makes so much of sin. We deny it, joke about it, even laugh about it because everyone does it to some degree. Many who believe sin to be a fact of life continue in it with little or no regard of its ultimate penalty.[23]

The God described in the Bible is one of not only abounding love, grace, holiness and mercy; but, He is also one of wrath, righteousness and judgment. He plans to expose all past wrongdoings on the last day when the Bible describes that we will tremble in His presence and all our thoughts and deeds will be exposed. God explains to man in His Word, the consequences of ignoring Him. He had the Bible written through various authors and has preserved it for all time so that men would have absolutely no excuse or be able to claim ignorance on Judgment Day. Even without a Bible, God has made Himself known through creation so that no one is excused, (see Romans 1:18-21.)

Regarding the Bible, many homes have one. Churches all over the world have Bibles available. One has even been placed by the Gideons in nearly every hotel room in America. Of course, one can be purchased at any bookstore or viewed for free on the internet. Bible studies can be found on Christian radio stations throughout the country and libraries contain Bibles and other helpful materials.

Have you ever been "evangelized?" Haven't you ever wondered why Christians try so hard to share the Gospel with the people they care about or why missionaries expose themselves to harsh living conditions in remote parts of the world, just to share the Gospel of Jesus with others who haven't heard?

Why would pastors devote their entire lives to preaching for a meager salary, and expend so much energy trying to reach others with what they know to be true? Why would anyone go knocking on doors and subject themselves to snickers and persecution? Why don't Christians just keep it to themselves, study their Bibles, and pray behind closed doors? It is simply because they are familiar enough with God's Word to be convinced of the extremely perilous situation others, who don't know God, will face at the end of their life on Earth. Lives are at stake and this is precisely why Jesus commands that Christians testify about Him and share the good news of salvation with others. As scary as it is, it is the loving thing to do.

Many people have heard of the final judgment and Hell but refuse to believe it could possibly be meant for them. This is an extremely dangerous presumption to make if based on feelings rather than on fact and verifiable evidence. According to the Bible, God has already cast a devastating judgment two recorded times in history. Archaeology has recently produced evidence for the devastating flood where God destroyed all mankind except Noah and his family. Archeology has also provided evidence that the cities of Sodom and Gomorrah were indeed demolished by some supernatural event.

How does the Bible describe Hell?

"For the cowardly and unbelieving......their place will be in the fiery lake of burning sulfur" (Revelation 21:8).

What is the alternative?

"Then I saw a new heaven and a new earth, for the first heaven and the first earth had passed away, and there was no longer any sea. I saw the Holy City, the new Jerusalem, coming down out of heaven from God, prepared as a bride beautifully dressed for her husband. And I heard a loud voice from the throne saying, 'Now the dwelling of God is with men, and he will live with them. They will be his people, and God himself will be with them and be their God. He will wipe every tear from their eyes. There will be no more death or mourning or crying or pain, for the old order of things has passed away'" (Revelation 21:1-4).

"The foundations of the city walls were decorated with every kind of precious stone...The twelve gates were twelve pearls...The street of the city was pure gold..." (Revelation 21:19-21) ... "To him who is thirsty I will give to drink without cost from the spring of the water of life. He who overcomes will inherit all this, and I will be his God and he will be my son" (Revelation 21:6).

If we believe in a God who is perfect and holy, then He must be perfectly just. Would it be fair if evil deeds went unpunished? Not at all. We all know how imperfect our court system is today in letting some guilty men free on technicalities of a complex court system. Some may even be set free if they falsely claim insanity. Others are able to convincingly evoke the sympathy of jurors by blaming society or their parents. Of course many who commit crimes simply don't get caught.

Who is going to vindicate the victims of guilty men and women who have managed to take advantage of our fallible justice system, which is run by fallible human beings? If a crime were left unpunished, our God would be less than perfect, wouldn't He? Therefore, as a just and righteous God, He has promised to avenge all wrongs when He returns.

I used to think that sin was relative and as long as I wasn't a murderer, a thief, or an adulterer and led a basically moral and upright life, then I would surely make it to heaven. Unfortunately, God does not grade on a curve, which is a very common misconception. We tend to rationalize our actions by comparing their severity with others. If our tendency to think in relative terms is in error, then how does the Bible define sin and what are the consequences?

In the Bible, God defines sin as rebellion against Him. In fact, it is simply *any* violation of His will. That's what the very first sin was all about. In the Garden of Eden, Adam and Eve were given one very specific command: They were not allowed to eat the fruit from one tree. I used to think, "What's the big deal in eating a piece of fruit?" I really didn't think that was a very serious sin at all. Why, then, were the resulting consequences so dire? This was the first time that God gave man an explicit directive and He didn't have to wait long to see what man would do. God simply waited to see whether the man would trust and obey Him, or not. Here, God gives the first man on Earth the opportunity to make a solemn decision which would change the world forever. Adam and Eve made the wrong choice and sinned simply by disobeying God. So the first sin committed must define the meaning of the word: any act that disobeys God.

When we disobey God, we selfishly put ourselves first and live the life He gave us any way we see fit. If that's all sin is, then we are all guilty and can be considered sinners.

The Bible clearly explains that, "There is no one righteous, not even one" (Romans 3:10).

"For all have sinned and fall short of the glory of God" (Romans 3:23).

"There is none who does good, not even one" (Psalm 14:3b).

What were the consequences for the rest of mankind? Death and suffering came into what was once a perfect world.

"For the wages [penalty] of sin is death" (Romans 6:23).

Since we are all sinners in God's eyes and doomed for eternal death, then man has a problem and a very serious one. The problem with relative thinking is that man's standard and God's standard are completely different. When we only compare ourselves to other people, we don't look so bad. But when we compare ourselves to God's holy standard, which He revealed to us in Jesus, we all fall far short of that standard.

The situation is this; God is holy. What does 'holy' mean? Among other things it means, 'perfect' and 'pure.' God is so holy, He can't be in the presence of sin. How, then, can we cross over the great chasm that separates us from God's holiness and our unholiness? God provided a way because it is His desire that none of us should perish. His desire is to have a relationship with His children so He provided a way that we could be redeemed.

"The Lord is not slack concerning his promise, as some men count slackness; but is longsuffering toward us, not willing that any should perish, but that all should come to repentance," (2 Peter 3:9).

This is why Jesus died on the cross and that although we were sick with sinfulness, "by His wounds we are healed." All we need to do is honestly believe and accept the offer of forgiveness. This is God's gift to all who will accept it. It is not automatic; it needs to be received by the individual and thus, we retain our freedom.

At the Last Supper Jesus said, "This is my blood of the new covenant which is poured out for many for the forgiveness of sins" (Matthew 26:28, Mark 14:24, Luke 22:20).

Note that in each Gospel account, the forgiveness is for 'many', not for *all* men. It is offered to every man, yet not all will accept it.

Jesus also said, "There is a judge for the one who rejects me and does not accept my words" (John 12:48).

Although it is God's desire that none of us perish, because He is perfect and just He still gives us choices to make. Ultimately, He proved the extent of His love for us by providing a remedy for sin, so that we could be redeemed, and friendship with Him could be restored forever. God declared to Moses and the Israelites in the Old Testament that the only adequate sacrifice was a blood sacrifice exchanging the blood of an innocent animal for man's sins. God gave the people very specific instructions regarding those animal sacrifices including when and how they were to be carried out. This was how God covered their sins that allowed His Spirit; then, to 'dwell' with them in the 'Ark of the Covenant' which they carried during their 40 years of desert wandering on the way to the Promised Land. Without the blood covering (or cleansing), a holy God could not have accompanied the Israelites on their way to the Promised Land.God often uses 'types' in His Word, which are pictures of things to come and that signify certain spiritual truths. It is a fascinating study which could fill volumes but we will explore just a few examples. Those animal sacrifices foreshadowed Christ's blood sacrifice, which would atone for the sins of all who would live after Jesus and follow Him.

The first Jewish Passover involved the sacrificial blood of a lamb and was the method by which the Jews would be protected from the final plague that God sent to the Egyptians under their King (Pharaoh). Pharaoh was ignoring all the miraculous warning signs God had given Moses to perform, thus refusing to believe and obey God's command to release the Jews from enslavement in Egypt.

As the tenth and final plague, an 'angel of death' was to come to Egypt and kill all the firstborn children and animals. God promised to protect each Jewish family who sacrificed a lamb which was perfect, a year old, and without any defects. They were to eat it that night and sprinkle the blood on the doorposts of their houses to escape the judgment that was visited on the Egyptians so that the angel would pass over them and not kill their firstborn.

> Now the LORD had said to Moses, "I will bring one more plague on Pharaoh and on Egypt. After that, he will let you go from here, and when he does, he will drive you out completely… Moses said "This is what the LORD says: 'About midnight…every firstborn son in Egypt will die …Tell the whole community of Israel that on the tenth day of this month, each man is to take a lamb…[which] must be year-old males without defect…Take care of them until the fourteenth day of the month, when all of the community of Israel must slaughter them at twilight. Then they are to take some of the blood and put it on the sides and tops of the doorframes of the houses where they eat the lambs…Eat it in haste; it is the LORD'S Passover'" (Exodus 11 and 12 excerpts).

It is a terrible thing to read but there was a great salvation for those who put their faith and trust in God and obeyed His command. The Jews have been celebrating this feast for thousands of years and still do to this day, yet some orthodox Jews have not made the connection between the blood of the lamb with the blood of Christ as atonement for their sin.

The firstborn lamb, which was without blemish, and its sacrificial blood, was the atonement for sin whereby the people would be delivered from slavery (which is the biblical symbol for sin). This was a crystal clear picture of Jesus Christ who was to come as the perfect lamb who would be slaughtered for the sins of mankind including the gentiles or non-Jews.

The Passover marked the Jew's deliverance from Egyptian slavery or 'bondage' and began their journey to the Promised Land, which 'flowed with milk and honey' and is analogous to heaven. The Bible says we are 'slaves to sin,' just as the Israelites were enslaved by the Egyptians and we have been delivered by sacrificial blood.

Jesus said, "I tell you the truth, everyone who sins is a slave to sin....if the Son sets you free, you will be free indeed" (John 8:34). Just as the symbolism of the Passover mirrored Christ's sacrifice and deliverance, slavery mirrors our bondage to sin, and the Promised Land mirrors heaven. There are countless other 'types' connecting the Old Testament to the New. Another example is Moses. He was the Jew's leader, teacher, and mediator in the Old Testament and while God spoke to the Jews through him, by faith, those who were obedient were saved. Jesus was the leader and teacher in the New Testament, and, through faith and obedience to Him we are saved.

In John Hagee's book, *The Beginning of the End*, he listed these astounding similarities between Moses and Jesus:

To be killed as infants	Exodus 1:15-17	Matthew 2:16
Parents saved their lives	Exodus 2:2-4	Hebrews 11:23
Protection found in Egypt	Exodus 2:10	Matthew 2:14-15
Meek and humble	Numbers 12:3	Matthew 11:28,30
Faithful to God	Numbers 12:7	Hebrews 3:1-6
Rejected by Israel	Exodus 2:13-14, 32:1	Matthew 27:21-22
Criticized by siblings	Numbers 12:1	John 7:5
Received by gentiles	Exodus 2:15, 21	Acts 13:44-48
Prayed God would forgive	Exodus 32:31-32	Luke 23:34
Willing to bear punishment	Exodus 32:31-32	1Peter 3:18
40 day desert fast	Exodus 34:28	Matthew 4:2
Spoke face to face with God	Numbers 12:7-8, Dt 34:10	John 1:18
Mountain commune w/God	Exodus 24:9-10	Matthew 17:1,5

Faces shown with glory	Exodus 34:34	Matthew 17:2
God spoke to from heaven	Exodus 19:19	John 12:23,28
Appeared alive after death		Matthew 17:3, John 20:19,20
Were teachers	Deuteronomy 4:1	John 3:1-2
Shepherds to God's people	Psalm 77:20	John 10:11-27
Revealed God's name	Exodus 3:13-14	John 17:6,11,12
Provided supernatural food	Exodus 16:14	Matthew 14:19,21
Brought deliverance	Exodus 3:7-8,10	Luke 4:17-19,21
Healed the people	Numbers 21:4-9	Matthew 4:23
Worked great miracles	Deuteronomy 34:10	Acts 2:22
Established a blood covenant	Exodus 24:7-8	Hebrews 9:11-15

Another 'type' is the covenant God made with Noah. A covenant in the Bible is a commitment. God made many covenants with his people and has sworn never to go back on His promises. God cannot lie and thus, has kept all of His vows with His people. One of the first covenants was with Noah. The world since Adam had become so wicked and perverse, that God destroyed all life with the exception of Noah, his family, and only two each of the entire animal kingdom.

> The LORD saw how great man's wickedness on the earth had become, and that every inclination of the thoughts of his heart was only evil all the time. The LORD was grieved that he had made man on the earth, and his heart was filled with pain. So the LORD said, "I will wipe mankind, whom I have created, from the face of the earth—men and animals, and creatures that move along the ground, and birds of the air—for I am grieved that I have made them." But Noah found favor in the eyes of the LORD (Genesis 6:5).

Only eight people: Noah, his wife, and his sons Shem, Ham, and Japheth with their wives, along with the animals were saved from the flood's devastation. The sign of the covenant is a rainbow so that all nations will remember God and the promise He made never again to destroy the earth by flood. The next time it will be by fire. I know it's hard to believe that Noah was the only righteous man on the entire earth, but such was the case. And so it was by faith and obedience that Noah and his family was spared.

Another covenant God made was with Abraham. He was to sacrifice his son Isaac on an altar and he obeyed.

This was yet another example of how God symbolically revealed the future sacrifice of His own Son. Abraham had enough faith and trust in God that he did as commanded. Just before the sacrifice, God stopped him and provided a substitute ram for the sacrifice. This is a picture of Christ, the substitute sacrifice for us. Abraham had successfully passed that test and because of his faith and obedience, God promised to give Abraham numerous descendants who would become the nation of Israel, and whom would inherit the Promised Land just as Christ's obedience obtained salvation for His own family of believers.

Since the time of Abraham and Moses it is unfortunate, that as each generation passed, the Israelites failed to maintain their faith. They became increasingly disobedient, immoral, and rebellious while turning to worship false gods. God had foreseen this rebellion and because He is faithful and never breaks a promise, He'd planned to establish a new covenant, which would be so significant an event that it would suffice until the end of time and atone for the sins of all whom would accept it. It was to be the sacrifice of all sacrifices. God himself came down to Earth and sacrificed Himself through His only son, Jesus Christ. It was not the blood of an animal lamb that would suffice; it was the blood of the perfect, firstborn, 'Lamb of God.' John the Baptist proclaimed, "Behold the Lamb of God, who takes away the sin of the world!" (John 1:29 ESV).

Once we accept the truth, confess our sins to God, repent, and commit to following His commands, we become children of God and coheirs of Christ's coming kingdom. From that point on anything we do to serve Christ, the King of the Jews and Gentiles, gets credited to our account where rewards according to our deeds will be given.

I had to ask myself some time ago, "What is the purpose of expending energy doing good deeds on Earth?" I had to ultimately admit that I was doing them to be liked, noticed, accepted, successful, all for my own selfish benefit and to 'glorify' myself. Why bother to store up rewards on Earth, which are not only minimal, but temporal as well? The alternative is to give all the glory to Christ by loving others and giving selflessly of ourselves in the name of Jesus. The result becomes a purpose on Earth to serve Christ out of love for Him and the rewards are not only spectacular, but also last for an eternity. In the process of Christ being accepted as truth through faith by an individual, God begins to perform a miraculous transformation within him. In the Bible, it is said God will, "turn a heart of stone into one of flesh" for those who are willing.

Although we will continue to sin because "it is in our nature to sin," we become able to recognize sin more quickly, and are motivated to turn away from it in obedience to God, whom we adore. Therefore, we welcome the change of our heart that God promises through His Holy Spirit and our lives should reflect this change of heart. As previously discussed, faith must be the starting point. The key is to try our best and confess when we fail although we will continue to sin.

The Apostle Paul wrote: "What I want to do I do not do, but what I hate I do.....I know that nothing good lives in me, that is, in my sinful nature. For I have the desire to do what is good, but I cannot carry it out" (Romans 7:15).

As long as we believe in Christ, confess our sins, and are truly repentant, we can have assurance of the promise of salvation.

"If you confess with your mouth, 'Jesus is Lord,' and believe in your heart that God raised Him from the dead, you will be saved" (Romans 10:9 ESV).

To summarize this section I'd like to point out the difference between one who has accepted and trusts in Christ, and one who has not. The Christian knows he is a sinner and recognizes his need for a Savior. He is aware that the ultimate penalty of unforgiven sin is eternal separation from God. Because of what Jesus accomplished on the cross, the Christian can be assured that all of his past and future sins are forgiven. As the Bible puts it, his debt has been paid in full by the blood of the Lamb.

The non-Christian does not recognize himself as a sinner and believes therefore, that he is in no need of a Savior. The non-Christian has no hope for eternal life while the Christian has tremendous hope all soundly based on God's promises; The Lord literally gave us 'His Word' and has a proven track record of keeping His promises. In addition, the Christian has purpose, joy, and peace in this life. He knows exactly where he came from, why he is here, and where he is going.

6

The Cross

God's plan is that the only way to eternal salvation is through His Son. Men have a major problem believing that all they need to do is believe this and trust His promises. It doesn't make sense to the average man that he doesn't have to do anything to earn his way into heaven (by doing good deeds, for example). God says that it is not possible for man to do or be good enough to meet His holy standards. It is in our nature to be selfish and to think of number one first. We put ourselves and desires above God's; that is our sinful nature.

The remedy for this sinfulness we tend toward is the sacrifice Jesus made on the cross. However, men have a difficult time accepting this truth or understanding it as God's plan. God anticipated that scholars and wise men would have a hard time accepting this reality and foretold it in His Word. The Apostle Paul wrote,

> For Christ didn't send me to baptize, but to preach the Gospel; and even my preaching sounds poor, for I do not fill my sermons with profound words and high sounding ideas, for fear of diluting the mighty power there is in the simple message of the cross of Christ. I know very well how foolish

it sounds to those who are lost, when they hear that Jesus died to save them. But we who are saved recognize this message as the very power of God. For God says, "I will destroy all human plans of salvation no matter how wise they seem to be, and ignore the best ideas of men, even the most brilliant of them."

So what about these wise men, these scholars, these brilliant debaters of this world's great affairs? God has made them all look foolish, and shown their wisdom to be useless nonsense. For God in his wisdom saw to it that the world would never find God through human brilliance, and then he stepped in and saved all those who believed his message, which the world calls foolish and silly. It seems foolish to the Jews because they want a sign from heaven as proof that what is preached is true; and it is foolish to the Gentiles because they believe only what agrees with their philosophy and seems wise to them.

So when we preach about Christ dying to save them, the Jews are offended and the Gentiles say it's all nonsense. But God has opened the eyes of those called to salvation, both Jews and Gentiles, to see that Christ is the mighty power of God to save them; Christ himself is the center of God's wise plan for their salvation. This so-called 'foolish' plan of God is far wiser than the wisest plan of the wisest man, and God in

> his weakness—Christ dying on the cross—is far stronger than any man (1 Corinthians 1:17-25 TLB).

This is sometimes referred to as 'The Great Exchange' where the One, perfect and sinless Christ took upon himself all the sins of those He would redeem (past present and future) and died while exchanging His life for ours. He was resurrected and by this He proved there is life after death if we put our trust in Him. Thus, He saved lives by giving His own as the payment for the penalty required by God for sin. Those who cannot bring themselves to be grateful for this incredible act of mercy will pay their penalty another way. The Bible is painfully clear on this point.

7

The Crucifixion

Many of us have been taught that Jesus suffered and died on a cross. This is certainly difficult and painful to imagine. What was it really like to be mocked, spit upon, beaten, nailed to a piece of wood, and left to suffocate to death?

Crucifixion was invented by the Persians between 300-400 B.C. It was 'perfected' by the Romans in the first century B.C. and is arguably the most painful death ever invented by man; this is where we get our term 'excruciating.' This particular form of torture and death was reserved primarily for the most vicious of criminals.

After Jesus' arrest He was spit upon, blindfolded, beaten, and flogged by the Roman guards. This process typically involved a whip with numerous leather thongs with bits of bone or glass embedded in the leather. According to Jewish custom a prisoner was usually flogged 39 times; forty minus one was a sign of Jewish mercy!

After these whippings the victim's skin was usually shredded, exposing underlying muscle and bone. After whipping Jesus mercilessly, the soldiers then beat him with their hands and with reeds. They proceeded to put a crown of thorns upon His head and finally crucified Him. This horrendous method of execution involved literally nailing the victim's hands and feet to a wooden crossbar. The crucifixion victim was pinned in such a way that it resulted in a very slow, painful death. As the person tried to bear his weight with his thigh muscles, they eventually collapsed flaccidly. Weight would shift to the arms and his shoulders would become dislocated. This made exhaling more difficult and breathing an impossibility. The heart rate increased and began to fail while the lungs filled with fluid. Blood loss and hyperventilation caused severe dehydration. This is probably why Jesus said, "I thirst." After several hours the victim suffocated to death.

When the Romans wanted to expedite the process, they would simply break the victim's legs, so that he could no longer support himself to inhale. Suffocation took place in a matter of minutes. At three o'clock, the afternoon of His death, Jesus said, "Tetelastai," which means, "It is finished." He then gave up His spirit. When the soldiers came to break His legs, they pierced His side to see if He was dead and out poured water and blood, indicating that He was in fact dead. It was not necessary to break his legs which fulfilled the prophecy, "Not one of His bones would be broken" (Psalm 34:20).

I realize it is difficult to read the details of Jesus' sufferings, yet, a full understanding of this sacrifice is necessary. This understanding should bring us to genuine sorrow for our sins, appreciation for what He has done, and is the first step toward true repentance and obedience. Was all this really necessary? According to God, it was.

A person must decide whether or not to accept and receive this gift which leads to eternal life. Some prefer to shut these events out of their minds and to live their life the way they see fit, thus ignoring God and what He did for them. It is the opinion of God that those people deserve the dire consequences of that decision which results in eternal separation from not only God but from those on Earth whom we loved and believed in Him. Is eternal punishment a fair and just consequence for simply not believing even though one has lived a basically moral and upright life? In the eyes of God, the answer is yes, because it is a blatant mockery of all Christ's sufferings, which we have just examined in detail. To do so is to laugh in the face of the Savior.

RESURRECTION—THE VICTORY:

The facts of Christ's death aren't amazing in themselves because many people in history were crucified. What is amazing is that Jesus rose from the dead! This is what makes all of His promises of eternal life a verifiable reality and this is the very heart of the claim of Christianity. Without the resurrection, there would be no hope of eternal life and Jesus would probably have gone down in the history books as just another prophet.

The fact is Jesus' tomb was found empty after three days and He emerged from the grave alive, just as He'd said He would. He made His first appearances to only a few, then, to hundreds. The book of 1Corinthians describes an appearance to a crowd of over 500 people. Paul wrote: "For I delivered to you as of first importance what I also received: that Christ died for our sins in accordance with the Scriptures, that he was buried, that he was raised on the third day in accordance with the Scriptures, and that he appeared to Cephas (Peter), then to the twelve. Then he appeared to more than **five hundred** brothers at one time, most of whom are still alive, though some have fallen asleep [died]. Then he appeared to James, then to all the apostles. Last of all, … he appeared also to me" (1Corinthians 1:3-8 ESV).

The Apostles weren't the only ones who recorded the historical event of the resurrection. Titus Flavius Josephus, a brilliant first century scholar, Jewish historian and not a Christian wrote the following in *Antiquities of the Jews*:

> At this time [the time of Pilate] there was a wise man who was called Jesus. His conduct was good and (he) was known to be virtuous. And many people from among the Jews and the other nations became his disciples. Pilate condemned him to be crucified and to die. But those who had become his disciples did not abandon his discipleship. They reported that he had appeared to them three days after his crucifixion, and that he was alive; accordingly he was perhaps the Messiah, concerning whom the prophets have recounted wonders (Book 18, Ch 3,Sec 3).

For 40 days following the resurrection, Christ walked with his disciples and taught them all they needed to know to firmly establish the Christian Church. Jesus showed them all of the prophecies that were written in the Old Testament hundreds of years before which foretold all of the details of Christ's life, death, resurrection, and future kingdom.

During that time, Jesus thoroughly instructed the apostles how to share the Good News of the Gospel and spread it throughout the world. He promised them He would always be with them "even until the end of the age" and later sent His Holy Spirit to them at Pentecost who was their counselor, comforter, and guide and reminded them of every word Jesus had spoken so they could accurately record it in their writings. Their task was to faithfully give their testimony as witnesses of all that Jesus did while He was on Earth which prove He was the Son of God. Then Jesus Christ ascended to heaven knowing that the foundation of His Church had been firmly established.

8

Faith And Love

In the beginning God created man to love and enjoy Him but, He determined that He will not force our love. He gave us the freedom to reject Him because love coerced is not freely given. He gives us just enough evidence to show us His power and goodness, yet not so much as to compel the unwilling. So He had a plan, even before the creation of the world, that provided man with the freedom to decide his own destiny.

Man, beginning with Adam, rebelled against God and did not return His love. To prove faithfulness and love for the Lord, God gave His chosen people, the Israelites, laws to follow. However, obeying out of fear instead of love was not powerful enough to overcome the temptation to do evil and they continued to rebel even serving other 'gods' whom they created for themselves.

Men did not recognize the extent of the love God had for His children so, God showed them by sending His only son to suffer and die for their rebellion. This was all pre-planned because God knows freedom has a cost, would involve a decision, and not all would receive Him. This was however, an opportunity for men to show the Lord true love out of appreciation for what He had done and for God to show men just how much He loves them.

You may be asking, "How has God actually demonstrated His incredible love for mankind?" Put simply, He literally came to Earth in the body of the man and Savior, Jesus Christ, who died on a cross and rose from the dead to rescue man from the punishment each deserves for his rebellion against God. He did this to show His great mercy and those who accept and receive this truth will be resurrected to joyously live with Him forever in a perfect world that man has always longed for.

Love is the most precious thing on earth. It is by far the most valuable thing we can have and enjoy with others. It is also the most powerful emotion on Earth. We know that from personal experience. More songs, poetry, and books have been written about love than on any other subject. You may have heard stories where a mother was able to lift the end of a car because her child was trapped underneath. That's power and it is highly motivating. Men and women have done extreme, often irrational things for the sake of loving another. The rage of a jealous person can drive him to do unspeakable deeds.

Most would agree that a man with all the money he could ever want is an empty and unfulfilled man without love in his life. It is surely more precious than gold or jewels. People marry for this reason; there is nothing more thrilling than the pure love shared between two people committed to each other for life. People have children for this reason as nothing can compare with a parent's love for his child and enjoying their love in return.

God showed us His unconditional and limitless love for us by sending Jesus to die for us so that we could have fellowship, in love, with Him, forever. This is why faith is so important. And not just faith in *something*, but faith and trust in the *person* of Jesus Christ. Once we believe in God, it makes us eager to learn more about Him which is why He gave us His Word. It shows us who He is, what He has done, how to love others, grow to maturity in our faith, how to endure life's difficulties, see what happens when we die, and describes our eternal home. As we study His Word, His love pours into us and it is irresistible when we contemplate the enormous sacrifice He made on our behalf. He has done it all and nothing we ever do could add to it. That is called grace, unmerited or undeserved favor for those who believe.

So it is faith and trust in Jesus that inspires genuine love for God and this love has the power to change our hearts not only toward Him but toward others also.

God foretold this through the prophet, Ezekiel, "I will give them one heart, and a new spirit I will put within them. I will remove the heart of stone from their flesh and give them a heart of flesh, that they may walk in my statutes and keep my rules and obey them. And they shall be my people, and I will be their God," (Ezekiel 11:19-20 ESV).

The Bible says, "The only thing that counts is faith expressing itself through love"(Galatians 5:6).

The Lord also said, "Love the Lord your God with all your heart and with all your soul and with all your mind and with all your strength" (Mark 12:30). Then He said, "Love your neighbor as yourself" (Mark 12:31).

Can someone command the love of another? What is usually the result of demanding that someone love you? Running away out of rebellion and fear would be the usual response. It is possible that this was the reason the Old Testament Covenant, which was centered on obeying a strict set of rules, had so little power. Maybe that was why the Israelites were so unsuccessful in pleasing God and were prone to worship idols.

When Jesus, who was God in the flesh, proved His love for us in such a remarkable way, men finally got the message and responded with true love out of appreciation for His forgiveness. That is the power of love and that is the response God seeks from His children. In addition, remember that God sent His followers the Holy Spirit. He is God "in us" who convicts us of sin, empowers us to refuse it and instructs us how to live *for* God and for the first time, not for ourselves and our own personal desires but selflessly putting others first.

Christianity has spread rapidly and forcefully ever since that particular gift was given to man. The fruit of a true disciple is genuine love for others with no expectation of earthly reward and explains why the first orphanages, hospitals, schools for all, including the blind and deaf, mission outposts, homeless shelters, humanitarian aid organizations (to name just a few) were founded by Christians. Jesus said that we prove we are His disciples if we bear righteous fruit: love, joy, peace, patience, goodness, faithfulness, gentleness, and self-control. There are others who claim to know God and produce a different kind of fruit: violence, murder, persecution, ignorance and pride. Jesus said we would know them by their fruit and indeed we can. This will be discussed later.

9

The Church

Jesus likened the church to a human body. The Christian church is a 'body' of believers and Christ is the head. He said the body is made up of many intricate parts each one as important as the other and all work together to make the entire unit function properly. He also said that when two or more are gathered in His name that He would be among them (Matthew 18:20).

The first disciples were called Christians in the city of Antioch which is in present day Turkey (Acts 11:26.) The members gathered together to hear the Apostles teach the words of Jesus, share in the Lord's Supper, worship God with songs and praise, pray for one another, encourage each other, and share possessions. It was and is really a *family* composed of children of God who each use their individual talents that God has given him or her in order to serve Him.

Paul wrote, "It was He who gave some to be apostles, some to be prophets, some to be evangelists, and some to be pastors and teachers, to prepare God's people for works of service, so that the body of Christ may be built up until we all reach unity in the faith and in the knowledge of the Son of God and become mature, attaining to the whole measure of the fullness of Christ" (Ephesians 4:11-13, Romans 12:4-6).

Paul said Christians share one Spirit and we are unified in faith and a true understanding of the Gospel. That is the good news that Christ died for us so that we could have the free gift of eternal life through God's grace and by His mercy.

David wrote we are to "Praise God in the congregation" (Psalm 68:26), "with songs" (v. 32), and "proclaim His power" (v. 34). Moses wrote we are to teach our children and grandchildren God's laws and instruct them how to live and behave (Ex18:20) and that we are to assemble to remember what God has done (Deuteronomy 4:9). It is also written that believers should not neglect meeting with one another to build one another up and encourage each other (Hebrews 10:25).

Churches should be filled with people whose hearts beat after God's and who's desire is to serve, honor, and praise Him for all He has done. That is the picture of true worship. Those who have put their trust in Christ have each been given one or more gifts for the purpose of serving God and advancing His Kingdom. In a search for the right church, someone may base his decision on what the church can do for him instead of what he can do for God. It is appropriate however, to look for a church that is faithfully teaching its members about God. It is impossible to "reach unity in the faith" if the people are not being taught who God really is which is only accomplished when a pastor teaches directly from the Bible.

One of the very last things Jesus said before he ascended to heaven was when He told Peter to feed His sheep (John 21:17). A pastor's calling then, is to feed his flock with spiritual food, which comes from the Word of God. In addition to the sermon, a solid Christian education program for adults and children should be offered as a means for them to grow in the knowledge of the Son of God, become mature, and equip the saints for service in and out of the actual church environment.

Some people therefore, have been given the gift to teach Bible studies. Others are gifted with beautiful voices to lead the songs, while some are talented carpenters who serve by building and maintaining the church. Others have been monetarily blessed and are the most able to contribute financially toward church maintenance, salaries, and the support of community outreach programs. In summary, church is not a place to simply expose our children in the hopes they will have a moral upbringing. It is also not intended to be used as an outward expression to others to 'prove' our Christianity. Nor was it intended to be a mysterious place of spiritual rituals where one goes through the motions of worship out of a sense of duty instead of worshipping from the heart. The church was founded as a place where one could sincerely express thankfulness to God. It is also a place where He is present and all have an opportunity to learn more about and thus, serve Him.

10

Religion Versus Christianity

There is a multitude of religions around the world, yet Christianity has withstood the test of time and is currently the world's largest religion. Most other religions have "prophets" who claim to have had revelations from God but what sets Christianity apart from all others is Jesus, the central figure. Only Christianity recognizes Jesus Christ as a deity himself, as God in human form. In addition, no other religious "prophet" performed the incredible miracles that Jesus did, including His resurrection from the dead, which as we have seen, was witnessed by many and thoroughly documented. This provides irrefutable evidence that He was in fact, sent by God as the Gospels record and that He was God in the flesh.

Most other religions teach that eternal life with God comes as the result of what *we* do on Earth in order to be accepted and admitted to heaven. Some examples are fasting, praying, sacrificing, being charitable, tithing, being circumcised, visiting Mecca (Muhammed's birthplace), and there are many others. Authentic Christianity relies on the truth of God's Word, which specifically states that a person is saved solely by the grace of God through an individual's faith in Jesus Christ. The way of salvation is by *His* deeds not ours. Once a person trusts Christ as his

Savior and acknowledges his need to be forgiven for sins (confession), then he vows to change his ways (repentance), and spends the rest of his days following Him in obedience. As we've said, God gives a person His Holy Spirit, who actually lives inside him, and this is what is meant by the term "born again." The person begins to change from the inside out by studying God's words and attempting to live by them; this process is called sanctification. Thus, Christianity is much more than just a religion, it's a life.

Jesus said, "Unless a man is born of water and the Spirit, he cannot enter the kingdom of God...You must be born again" (John 3:5-7).

Let's review exactly what it means to be "born again" as described in The Bible. This is such a widely misunderstood term, I felt it would be helpful to explain where the term originated and what it means.

The phrase originated with Jesus himself in a conversation He had with a man named Nicodemus who was a high profile, religious leader and had devoted his entire life to serving God (Yahweh) as a Jewish rabbi. Regardless of a life devoted to God, it is obvious in this exchange that Nicodemus (and Jews in general) didn't have any idea what it really meant to know God in a personal way and that in order to love and serve him faithfully, he must receive a new heart and spirit which would only be given to those who have faith and trust in the Son.

Nicodemus, like the other Sadducees and Pharisees, thought he was faithfully serving God through religious rituals and traditions. This is what all other religions do; they teach man-made rules and traditions treating God's Word as incomplete and insufficient. Jesus told the Jewish leaders that they were actually rejecting God's commands in order to keep their traditions (Mark 7:9).

It is interesting that Nicodemus approached Jesus in the middle of the night with his questions. Perhaps he did not want to be seen by his contemporaries who were greatly irritated that Jesus had arrived on their 'religious' scene and was turning the Jewish world upside down with His teaching.

The biblical passage where Jesus makes it clear that a person must be born again to enter the Kingdom of God can be found in John 3:

> Now there was a man of the Pharisees named Nicodemus, a member of the Jewish ruling council. He came to Jesus at night and said,
>
> "Rabbi, we know you are a teacher who has come from God. For no one could perform the miraculous signs you are doing if God were not with him." In reply Jesus declared, "I tell you the truth, no one can see the kingdom of God unless he is born again."
>
> "How can a man be born when he is old?" Nicodemus asked. "Surely he cannot enter a second time into his mother's womb to be born!" Jesus answered, "I tell you the truth, no one can enter the kingdom of God unless he is born of

> water and the Spirit. Flesh gives birth to flesh, but the Spirit gives birth to spirit. You should not be surprised at my saying, 'You must be born again'"... "How can this be?" Nicodemus asked. "You are Israel's teacher," said Jesus, "and you do not understand these things?"

Jesus appears perplexed (but not really surprised) with this so-called 'religious' leader who did not understand what Jesus was talking about. As an Old Testament 'expert,' one would expect Nicodemus to immediately recall Ezekiel 36:25 where the Lord says, "I will sprinkle clean water on you, and you will be clean; I will cleanse you from all your impurities and from all your idols. I will give you a new heart and put a new spirit in you; I will remove from you your heart of stone and give you a heart of flesh. And I will put my Spirit in you and move you to follow my decrees and be careful to keep my laws."

As a teacher, the Jewish people were dependent upon Nicodemus for sound theological instruction and Jesus seemed somber that Nicodemus was unfamiliar with this Old Testament prophecy. During their short exchange, Jesus references the "new birth" not once, but five times to stress its significance. He makes the firm statement that "no one" can enter the Kingdom of God unless he is born again.

The Spirit of God guides us, instructs us, and produces a positive change within us. It is an awesome experience to watch a person change from being selfish, bitter, unforgiving, and critical to one who grows into a beautiful human being as a direct result of trust in Jesus Christ and accepting His new heart. I have observed this miracle more than once and I am convinced only the power of God could accomplish such a feat. The Bible says, "If anyone is in Christ, he is a new creation; the old has gone, the new has come! All this is from God" (2 Corinthians 5:17 ESV).

It is clear that one must make a conscious decision to believe in Jesus and to receive Him by asking him to come into a person's life.

John 1:12 states, "But as many as received Him, to them He gave the right to become children of God."

And Paul, "If you confess with your mouth that Jesus is Lord and believe in your heart that God raised him from the dead, you will be saved. For with the heart one believes and is justified, and with the mouth one confesses and is saved" (Romans 10:9-10 ESV).

I need to avoid a misunderstanding at this point. Although an individual receives and confesses Christ, salvation of souls is not under any one person's control. God says in His Word that He is the one who initiates a person's call toward Christ and that it is the Father who 'draws' him (John 6:44), but that is an entirely different subject altogether which I won't elaborate on at this time. The best resource I have read on the subject of God's sovereignty is *Foundations of Grace* by Steven J. Lawson.

Moving along, it is obviously not enough just to intellectually believe in Jesus; even the Pharisees believed

He had done great miracles. It is also not enough to be a 'good' person. Finally, it is not enough to be raised in a particular church and practice 'religion by rote' where one must follow rigorous rules and receive various sacraments to be in good standing with God and the church leaders. That is exactly what the Pharisees were doing and they were severely criticized by Jesus himself. They were suffocating the people with their rules and placing a heavy burden on them.

Jesus said, "My yoke is easy and my burden is light" (Matthew 11:30).

We will never get to heaven on our own no matter how good we try to be. Only belief in Christ can give us that assurance and peace.

Jesus said, "Beware of the teachers of the law. They like to walk around in flowing robes and love to be greeted in the marketplaces and have the most important seats in the synagogues...for a show they make lengthy prayers. Such men will be punished most severely" (Luke 20:46-47).

The type of belief the Bible talks about involves a simple, personal acceptance, which is between God and the individual alone. It is not ceremonial, nor requires any grand announcement. It is as simple as a quiet prayer. A person confesses to God that he is sinful and desires forgiveness. He truly believes that Christ is the one whom God provided to suffer in that person's place and who would not only spare the person from eternal damnation but also promise him eternal life in heaven.

Once born again, although we may have adult bodies, we become 'spiritual' children who are starting life all over again. From this time on, we know our Father and let Him guide us and we begin to see the world through His eyes instead of our own. It is an attitude adjustment where we think of others more than ourselves. We are given a new purpose and the previous life's uncertainties are now easily explained. Once this is understood, the new birth makes sense. This offer is for all who will accept it and God promises not to turn anyone away.

Jesus said, "All that the Father gives me will come to me, and whoever comes to me I will never drive away. For I have come down from heaven not to do my will but to do the will of him who sent me. And this is the will of him who sent me, that I shall lose none of all that he has given me, but raise them up at the last day. For my Father's will is that everyone who looks to the Son and believes in him shall have eternal life, and I will raise him up at the last day" (John 6:37-40).

For those seeking to know more details, the next logical steps would be to read the Bible, particularly the Gospels, and seek out a Bible-teaching church that offers Bible classes in addition to their worship services. Ongoing Bible study is crucial for understanding God's plan for you and the world as a whole.

11

The End Times

What signs did Jesus say would indicate the imminent approach of His return to Earth followed by the end of the world, as we know it? The disciples asked Him, "What will be the sign of Your coming and of the end of the age?" Jesus answered that false prophets would come, Christians would be hated, persecuted, and killed. Sin would increase and love would grow cold. Wars would rage, famines, disease, and earthquakes would increase. Many would turn from the truth toward fables and be led astray and the Gospel would be preached throughout the entire world (Matthew 24).

I would say that picture paints the world today very accurately. All aspects of this prophecy are certainly on the increase, particularly the violence and the devaluation of human life. All one has to do is listen to the news. Organizations are begging for money to help starving children, disabled veterans, displaced refugees, and to find cures for all types of disease. Even as I write these words a devastating pandemic is killing thousands across the globe. The Coronavirus (COVID-19), has infected over six million people and killed over 371,000. Many are estimating over 15 million people will die. The greatest world economies are toppling under the strain as people are ordered to stay at home while only essential businesses remain open.

Wars rage, greedy dictators force teen children to sell 'favors' for food, and politicians argue for 'women's rights' condoning the murder of unborn babies. Nations spend so much on nuclear programs that the civilians are dying of starvation while food and water supplies worldwide continue to rapidly decrease. Natural and geophysical disasters have steadily increased in recent decades and according to EM-DAT, (The International Disaster Database for the U.N. with the most detailed disaster data available in the world), there have been 22,000 mass natural disasters in the world from 1900 to the present. Data prior to 1900 is difficult to obtain but two trend statistics report there were 78 disasters in 1970 which jumped to 348 in 2004 and from 1980 to 2009 there has been an 80 percent increase in climate-related disasters. There are other signs of the end times described in the Bible.

Paul describes society today vividly and accurately, "There will be terrible times in the last days. People will be lovers of themselves, lovers of money, boastful, proud, abusive, disobedient to their parents, ungrateful, unholy, without love, unforgiving, slanderous, without self control, brutal, not lovers of the good, treacherous, rash, conceited, lovers of pleasure rather than lovers of God—having a form of godliness but denying its power… They are the kind who worm their way into homes and gain control over weak willed women, who are loaded down with sins and are swayed by all kinds of evil desires, always learning but never able to acknowledge the truth" (2 Timothy 3:1-7).

What has happened to our society as a result of men becoming 'lovers of themselves, lovers of money, and lovers of pleasure?' Has civilization bred more civilized people or are things escalating for the worse? We are surely lovers of money. The first news many want to hear when they turn on the radio or television is how the Dow Jone's Industrial average is fairing. It has become the top news report of the day. Divorce rates have skyrocketed and at some weddings the vows being read have changed from "as long as we both shall *live*" to "as long as we both shall *love*." The mentality is that a life long commitment is not appropriate. People simply divorce when the love wears off. Crime is not only on the rise but the types of crimes being committed are monstrous.

Think of the change that has occurred in just the last fifty years. Many people rarely locked their doors yet, today a security system is practically a necessity. My family used to leave our car unlocked with the keys in the ignition; I'd be a fool to do such a thing today. My brothers and sisters and I would play outside in the woods, in the neighborhood, at the nearby lake, etc. and be gone all day until dinnertime. Today, if I were to leave my children in the car while I stopped for milk, I would likely be charged with negligence and could lose custody of them! I can't even let them go to the bus stop (which is at my front curb) or into a restaurant bathroom unsupervised for fear someone may abduct them.

Because of the number of divorces and an obsession with money, I believe the children suffer the most. Many are in total, hopeless despair, which has escalated teen suicides, drug use, and alcoholism. Depressed people lash out by shooting crowds of innocent people at concerts, schools, places of worship, marketplaces, and entertainment venues.

The level of violence in the hearts of men today is absolutely unreal: bombings, burning churches, individual and mass murders, child molestation, gross mutilations, human trafficking, etc. The list is endless. Jesus said, "...then many will be offended, will betray one another, and will hate one another...and because lawlessness will abound, the love of many will grow cold" (Matthew 24:10-12).

Surely, the evidence reveals that the love of many has grown cold; their blood runs cold as ice as 'hearts are turned to stone.' We have always had violence, but, what is absolutely terrifying, is the increase of murders committed by children. These youths have absolutely no regard for the value of a human life. They commit horrendous crimes for no apparent reason and without a shred of remorse. They are our next generation.

Where will it all lead? Where are we headed? Is the world situation getting better or increasingly worse? Nothing seems to shock us anymore. The question is, when will God have had enough? How long will He allow these things to persist? When will His 'cup of wrath' be full?

God said, "Doom has come upon you—you who dwell in the land. The time has come, the day is near; there is panic, not joy, upon the mountains. I am about to pour out my wrath on you and spend my anger against you" (Ezekiel 7:7-8).

"When the Son of Man comes in his glory, and all the angels with him, he will sit on his throne in heavenly glory. All the nations will be gathered before him, and he will separate the people one from another as a shepherd separates the sheep from the goats. He will put the sheep on his right and the goats on his left. Then the King will say to those on his right, 'Come, you who are blessed by my Father; take your inheritance, the kingdom prepared for you since the creation of the world.'.... Then he will say to those on his left, 'Depart from me, you who are cursed, into the eternal fire prepared for the devil and his angels.' Then they will go away to eternal punishment, but the righteous to eternal life" (Matthew 25:31-34,41,46).

Men cry out for justice today. We all know that our courts, judges, and lawyers have become so corrupt that there is rarely true justice. He who has the most money often wins in court. There will certainly be justice; the evil that abounds will not go unpunished according to Jesus.

The Bible is very specific about this, "The Lord looked and was displeased that there was no justice....According to what they have done, so will He repay wrath to His enemies and retribution to His foes" (Isaiah 59:15,18).

One final sign of the end is this: "This gospel of the kingdom will be preached in all the world, as a witness to all the nations, and then the end will come" (Matthew 24 :14).

Thanks to worldwide evangelists and missionaries, this prophecy is being rapidly fulfilled today. For only a matter of decades have radio, television, and air travel afforded its world citizens the ability to fulfill this prophecy. With the explosion and availability of personal computer use, an extraordinary means of reaching people throughout the world via the Internet, Christian chat groups, and e-mail has become reality. For the first time in history evangelical broadcasters now reach every language group in the world and according to the 2019 Wycliff Global Alliance Bible Translation Statistics, "As of October 2019 the full Bible has been translated into 698 languages, the New Testament has been translated into an additional 1,548 languages and Bible portions or stories into 1,138 other languages. Thus at least some portions of the Bible have been translated into 3,385 languages."

The growth of the Christian church in the last century has been astonishing. Since 1949 the number of Christians in communist China has escalated from just one million to 60-80 million and despite terrible persecution there are between 10,000-25,00 converts per day.

By 1900 only three percent of Africans had accepted Christ despite dedicated missionary efforts. In the last 90 years, however, over 50% of the 1.2 billion citizens of

Africa have embraced Christ as their Lord and Savior. It has been estimated that more than 85,000 people accept Christ as their Savior every day throughout the world. The number of Christians in Indonesia has increased from 1.3 million in 1980 to 11 million today. Until 1960 Christianity was prohibited in Nepal and currently there are over 500,000 believers and a church in every one of the country's 75 districts. In Iran (one of the top ten persecutors of Christians in the world), approximately 500 Muslims convert to Christianity every month. Every day in Asia 50,000 people served by *Asia Access* come to Christ. In the last 100 years the number of Christians in the world has quadrupled from 600 million to over two billion.

In light of all these statements made by Jesus concerning the signs of the end, it certainly appears He will be coming soon. The question that needs to be addressed is,

"Are you ready?"

12

God's Plan

God's plan for His children is thoroughly explained in the Bible. It contains answers to the many questions a man might think to ask in his lifetime. In it, God arms us with the full knowledge of who we are, how we got here, why we are here, and where we are going.

The Israelites were chosen as a specific group of people through whom God would reveal Himself and His awesome plan, which applies to all mankind. The Lord instructs us, disciplines us, and reveals His character to us in His Book. Through the events of history, as recorded in the Bible, God shows He is the creator of all things, which unmistakably reveals His majesty. It shows us He is in control of all things; He is sovereign. It shows us that He sees all things and that he knows every thought and deed of every man; He is omniscient.

We are His children and He is our Father. Imagine the love a parent has for a child and multiply that a million times over. It would still not come close to the love He has for us, His precious children. Does a child do anything to deserve or earn his parent's unconditional love? No, and neither do God's children. It is freely given by a parent just as it is a free gift from our heavenly Father. All God wants is for his children to acknowledge who He is, accept His love, to believe, and to trust in Him. It is to trust in His promises to provide, protect, answer our prayers, and to give eternal life.

I find it intriguing that small children readily accept that God created everything and is constantly watching over us. It is sad that as we grow up, we let the opinions of others talk us out of what we already knew as children to be true.

As we have seen, all sin is simply a lack of faith and willful disobedience to His call to draw close to him. He offers us everything a man could desire and more: protection, love, blessings, and even eternal life with Him as one of His family. How painful it must be when with this gift that He was gracious enough to give, results in a decision to push away from all the love and blessings He offers and basically say to His face, “I don’t want you!” It is to say, “I want to take the life you have given me and live it my own way!”

How gracious it is that God would pursue us our entire life even after that rejection and that He will forgive us at any moment if we would only respond to His call in confession and repentance. What incredible love and patience He has!

However unbelievable it sounds, it makes total sense to me when I consider how we deal with our own children. When they are obedient, we live in peace and harmony. When they are disobedient, do we stop loving them? Of course not. We have even greater compassion because they are miserable and don’t know what’s best for them (although they think they do)! Suppose one was to run away from home; wouldn't we be standing at the very door waiting with open arms if they would decide to return?

We show our children love through discipline, which is a clear signal to them that we care about their well being. Following the rebellious struggles children experience growing up, with the right amount of love, they are prepared to grow into mature adults ready to face the world, start their own families, and repeat the process with their own children.

The entire biblical history of the Israelites is a clear reflection of our own lives. God was revealed to the Jews through visitations of angels, incredible miracles, and prophets revealing His will. God said about the Israelites, "they are rebellious, hard-headed, and stiff-necked."

But God never stopped loving them and drawing them back to Him just as most of us would do with our own children. The Israelites drew close and followed His commands, and then they turned and worshipped a golden calf in place of Him. They grumbled and whined in the desert not believing He would provide food and water but then He did provide for them. They didn't trust God would win their battles for them while on the journey into the Promised Land but He did see that they were successful in their battles. Each time they pulled away, they were disciplined by their Father and they repented a greater amount each time drawing closer and closer to trusting, and thus, believing in Him.

The Israelites' journey with God is intended as a model for all of us. We can observe their successes, failures, rebellion, and the consequences of both obedience and disobedience. It was surely God's design that we are to learn from their cyclical history of trusting, then rebelling, being disciplined, then trusting again, and turning to repentance and obedience.

As persistently rebellious as we are, God continues to reveal Himself in a multitude of ways. We fight it in utter disbelief that someone could love us so much despite that we have nothing to offer in return. We feel that love has to be conditional because we have learned to love and give love that way. We think to ourselves, "I can only love you if you fulfill my needs. I can't love a person if he isn't tender, compassionate, or if we have nothing in common."

Don't we tend to love others based on what they can do for us or how well they fulfill our emotional and physical needs? Don't we determine whether we are capable of being loved by another by how well we feel we can meet their needs? That is conditional love and we all exhibit it except with our own children. Somehow, we are able to love them no matter what. That is the love of God and He gave us that capability to love our children in a like manner. I believe that is one way that we were made "in His image" (Genesis 1:26).

If you are a parent, what would be the ultimate proof that you love your child? Would you be willing to sacrifice your life for that little one's if you had to? Imagine yourself in a tragic situation where it was your life or your child's. Let's say you and your child are on the 14th floor of a burning hotel building. The rescue helicopter is outside the window and there is only room for one more person. Would you climb aboard the craft and leave your baby behind or would you hand him over with a kiss, knowing it will be too late to save you when the chopper returns?

As the final, climactic, and demonstrative proof of God's love for each of His children, He was willing to come down to Earth from His comfortable throne, in extremely humble circumstances, in the human body of Jesus Christ to ultimately give His life for ours. Jesus tirelessly worked with the disciples for three years teaching and fully revealing Himself and His redemptive plan, which He has been working out for us all along. Then after the crucifixion and resurrection, as we have learned, he spent 40 days with the disciples teaching them all they needed to know about the Kingdom of God and how they were to help build it.

Luke wrote, "In my former book, Theophilus, I wrote about all that Jesus began to do and to teach until the day he was taken up to heaven, after giving instructions through the Holy Spirit to the apostles he had chosen. After his suffering, he showed himself to these men and gave many convincing proofs that he was alive. He appeared to them over a period of forty days and spoke about the kingdom of God" (Acts 1:1-4).

As we watch God's plan unfold, we would be naturally curious how it all ends and where we are in redemptive history. In the next chapter we will review just how the Bible reveals the last part of God's plan and how it will be played out in its final stages.

13

What Happens Next

Most people who believe in God are familiar with the idea of a final judgment. I had always been under the impression that sometime after death we would stand before God, be judged guilty or innocent, then proceed to our final destination: heaven or hell. I had never heard of the Second Coming of Jesus Christ and His plans to come back to earth.

The book of Revelation, written by the apostle John, is the last book of the Bible which gives the most detail of this and other final events; however, the symbolic imagery used can be difficult to interpret, but the necessary, overall message is unmistakably clear.

In the New Testament, Jesus himself explains that He will come again personally, bodily, and visibly. At His appearance, all believers in Him, whether dead or alive, will be taken from the earth (or resurrected) and will be given a new body.

"For the Lord himself will come down from heaven, with a loud command, with the voice of the archangel and with the trumpet call of God, and the dead in Christ will rise first. After that, we who are still alive and are left will be caught up together with them in the clouds to meet the Lord in the air. And so we will be with the Lord forever" (1 Thessalonians 4:16).

"Listen, I tell you a mystery: We will not all sleep, but we will all be changed— in a flash, in the twinkling of an eye, at the last trumpet. For the trumpet will sound, the dead will be raised imperishable, and we will be changed. For the perishable must clothe itself with the imperishable, and the mortal with immortality. When the perishable has been clothed with the imperishable, and the mortal with immortality, then the saying that is written will come true: 'Death has been swallowed up in victory. Where, O death, is your victory? Where, O death, is your sting?'" (1 Corinthians 15:51).

"Two men will be in the field; one will be taken and the other left. Two women will be grinding with a hand mill; one will be taken and the other left" (Matthew 24:40-41).

THE DATE AND TIME UNKNOWN

Jesus said many times that no one would know the time or day of this Second Coming, "No one knows about that day or hour, not even the angels in heaven, nor the Son, but only the Father. As it was in the days of Noah, so it will be at the coming of the Son of Man. For in the days before the flood, people were eating and drinking, marrying and giving in marriage, up to the day Noah entered the ark; and they knew nothing about what would happen until the flood came and took them all away. That is how it will be at the coming of the Son of Man…Therefore keep watch, because you do not know on what day your Lord will come" (Matthew 24:36-42). The apostle Paul wrote, "Now, brothers, about times and dates we do not need to write to you, for you know very well that the day of the Lord will come like a thief in the night. While people are saying, 'Peace and safety,' destruction will come on them suddenly…" (1Thessalonians 5:1-3).

THE EARTH WILL BE DESTROYED BY FIRE

"The day of the Lord will come like a thief. The heavens will disappear with a roar; the elements will be destroyed by fire, and the earth and everything in it will be laid bare… That day will bring about the destruction of the heavens by fire, and the elements will melt in the heat. But in keeping with his promise we are looking forward to a new heaven and a new earth, the home of righteousness" (2 Peter 3:10-13).

"This is the plague with which the LORD will strike all the nations that fought against Jerusalem: Their flesh will rot while they are still standing on their feet, their eyes will rot in their sockets, and their tongues will rot in their mouths. On that day men will be stricken by the LORD with great panic. Each man will seize the hand of another, and they will attack each other" (Zechariah 14:12).

This sounds oddly like what happens to the bodies of human beings who are exposed to the sweeping, all-consuming, radioactive wave from the blast of a nuclear bomb. We live in a world where, the threat of a nuclear holocaust is a very real possibility. In addition, the final plagues described in Revelation could easily be the physical effects of chemical and biological weapons of mass destruction.

"The first angel went and poured out his bowl on the land, and ugly and painful sores broke out on the people who had the mark of the beast and worshiped his image" (Revelation 16:2).

THE GREAT WHITE THRONE JUDGMENT

"Then I saw a great white throne and him who was seated on it. Earth and sky fled from his presence, and there was no place for them. And I saw the dead, great and small, standing before the throne, and books were opened. Another book was opened, which is the book of life. The dead were judged according to what they had done as recorded in the books...each person was judged according to what he had done....If anyone's name was not found written in the book of life [believers in Jesus], he was thrown into the lake of fire" (Revelation 20:11-15).

THE NEW HEAVEN AND NEW EARTH

People have interesting thoughts about heaven. Many picture it as a place in the clouds with angels, in disembodied spirits with harps, singing, and basically, endless boredom. Nothing could be further from the truth. Not, at least, as God describes it.

> Then I saw a new heaven and a new earth, for the first heaven and the first earth had passed away, and there was no longer any sea. I saw the Holy City, the new Jerusalem, coming down out of heaven from God, prepared as a bride beautifully dressed for her husband. And I heard a loud voice from the throne saying, "Now the dwelling of God is with men, and he will live with them. They will be his people, and God himself will be with them and be their God.
>
> He will wipe every tear from their eyes. There will be no more death or mourning or crying or pain, for the old order of things has passed away." He who was seated on the throne said, "I am making everything new!" Then he said, "Write this down, for these words are trustworthy and true" (Revelation 21:4).

The Bible explains that God will redeem not only mankind so He can live with him, but that He will redeem the earth as well. Man's habitation on Earth has certainly taken its toll, ecologically speaking. We have abused what we were given and in our industrial greed, we have depleted our natural resources and irresponsibly polluted the air, earth, and sky. The Bible indicates that God will make all things new again, perhaps as they were in the Garden of Eden.

When we receive our new, incorruptible bodies that will never see weakness or disease, we will play, laugh, sing, dance, work, learn, travel, eat, drink, worship and discover God's marvelous creation the way He originally designed it *before* sin entered the world. I believe animals will be present also because they are the most creative and fascinating of all God's handiwork. Why else would He have been so careful to include pairs of every species in the ark? In addition, He knows we love and would miss our beloved pets who were, after all, innocent casualties of man's fall. I believe we will be thrilled with what is in store. God said, "What no eye has seen, nor ear heard, nor the heart of man imagined, what God has prepared for those who love him" (1 Corinthians 2:9 ESV).

What an awesome promise!

"He said to me: 'It is done. I am the Alpha and the Omega, the Beginning and the End. To him who is thirsty I will give to drink without cost from the spring of the water of life. He who overcomes will inherit all this, and I will be his God and he will be my son. But the cowardly, the unbelieving, the vile, the murderers, the sexually immoral, those who practice magic arts, the idolaters and all liars—their place will be in the fiery lake of burning sulfur'" (Revelation 21:6).

Jesus said, "Behold, I am coming soon! My reward is with me, and I will give to everyone according to what he has done. I am the Alpha and the Omega, the First and the Last, the Beginning and the End" (Revelation 22:12-13).

14

Summary

The Gospel message is incredibly simple. So simple, in fact, that even a child can understand it. This "Good News" can be summarized in a single paragraph.

As sinners, we all face the grave. Following our physical death, there will be a judgment which will result in an eternity of either an indescribably joyful life with God our Father or separation from Him in suffering forever. The latter would be the result of a devastating mistake of choice during our life on Earth. The "Great Exchange" God made for us out of His mercy on us was to take every single one of our individual sins and place them on a perfect, sinless Jesus Christ. All those sins were then put to death with Him on the cross and out of God's sight forever so that we would be pleasing and acceptable to Him as was originally intended.

God is offering each of us eternal life; the most valuable and desired gift a man could ever wish for and it is free. The only requirement is to receive Jesus Christ into your heart and follow Him, no matter the cost.

It is my sincerest hope and prayer that this manuscript will help you make the single, most important decision you will ever make in your life: to follow God's way, or to go your own way and risk the consequences. If you have read this far, at least you can make an informed choice in this matter.

When we honestly evaluate and weigh the evidence set before us: the wonders of creation, the authenticity of the Bible, fulfilled prophecy, and Jesus' living testimony, I feel that the scales are heavily tipped in favor of the claims of Christianity.

There is obviously a mound of evidence to be considered and I hope this has been an informative introduction on the subject. One will never have 100% proof as that would leave no room for faith. There are some excellent materials available for further research, which can be found at any Christian or online bookstore. Some of my personal favorites are listed in the bibliography. Continue to search with an open mind; you will find your answers. In closing, here are just a few of the promises God has made to those who are searching for answers with an open heart.

"Ask and it will be given to you; seek and you will find; knock and the door will be opened to you. For everyone who asks receives; he who seeks finds; and to him who knocks, the door will be opened" (Matthew 7:7).

"And without faith it is impossible to please God, because anyone who comes to Him must believe that He exists and that He rewards those who earnestly seek Him" (Hebrews 11:6).

I would like to conclude with the promise Jesus made to those who would accept Him as their Lord and Savior, "Here I am! I stand at the door and knock. If anyone hears my voice and opens the door, I will go in and eat with him, and he with me. To him who overcomes, I will give the right to sit with me on my throne, just as I overcame and sat down with my Father on his throne. He who has an ear, let him hear..." (Revelation 3:20).

APPENDIX A

NOTES

1. Robert Jastrow, *God and the Astronomers*, (W.W. Norton & Co. N.Y., 2000), 15-16.
2. Hugh Ross, "Probability for a Life Support Body," Appendix B, *Lights in the Sky and Little Green Men* (Colorado Springs, CO: NavPress, 2002).
3. Laura Z. Powell, "Made for Me: The Design Argument," May 28,2019, www.laurazpowell.org.
4. Roy Abraham Varghese, ed., *The Intellectuals Speak Out About God,* (Chicago Regnery Gateway, 1984), 25-26.
5. Grant Jeffrey, *The Handwriting of God* (Frontier Research Publications, Inc., 1997), 239.
6. Michael Denton, *Evolution: A Theory in Crisis* (Bethesda, Md.: Adler & Adler, 1985), 264.
7. Behe, *Darwin's Black Box: The Biochemical Challenge to Evolution* (New York: Touchstone, 1996), 232-233.
8. Jeffrey, *The Handwriting of God*, 223.
9. Jeffrey, *The Handwriting of God*, 221.
10. Charles Darwin, *The Origin of Species* (London. J.M. Dent & Sons LTD., 1971) 167.
11. Denton, *Evolution: A Theory in Crisis*, 245.
12. J.B. Birdsell, *Human Evolution* (Chicago: Rand McNally, 1972), 141.

13. N.O. Newell, "Adequacy of the Fossil Record," Journal of Paleontology, Vol.33, May 1959), 492.
14. Derek Ager, *Principles of Paleoecology* (San Francisco: McGraw-Hill Book Co., 1963), 249.
15. Charles Schuchert and Carl Dunbar, *Textbook of Geology Pt.2*, (New York: John Wiley & Sons, 1933), 212.
16. Derek Ager, *Principles of Paleoecology*, 108.
17. Duane T. Gish, *Evolution: The Fossils Still Say No!* (El Cajon, CA.: Institute For Creation Research, 1995), 326.
18. Gareth Nelson, *Lucy's Child* (New York: William Morrow and Co., 1989), 74.
19. Wynn Kenyon, Article: "Living in a Material World" (Table Talk Magazine, Nov issue, 1998 Ligonier Ministries and R.C. Sproul).
20. Josh McDowell, *More Than a Carpenter* (Living Books, 1986), 48.
21. Kenneth Boa & Larry Moody, *I'm Glad You Asked* (David C.Cook,1995), 81.
22. Oswald Chambers, *My Utmost For His Highest* (Barbour & Co., Inc. 1963), 206.
23. Porter Barrington, *The Christian Life New Testament Master Outlines and Study Notes* (Thomas Nelson Publishers, 1982), 432.
24. Bruce R. McConkie, *Mormon Doctrine*, (Bookcraft Co. 1958), 670.
25. The Articles of Faith of the Church of Christ of Latter Day Saints, Ch 1 Section 8.
26. Brigham Young, *Journal of Discourses*, (Liverpool: ASA Calkin), 6:229, 7:289.

Appendix B

Suggested Reading

I Don't Have Enough Faith to Be an Atheist, Norman L. Geisler & Frank Turek

Halley's Bible Handbook, H.H. Halley

The Christian Life New Testament With Master Outlines and Study Notes, Porter Barrington

The Holiness of God, R.C. Sproul

The Lie: Evolution, Ken Ham

I'm Glad You Asked, Kenneth Boa & Larry Moody

More Than a Carpenter, Josh McDowell

Evidence Demands a Verdict, Josh McDowell

When Skeptics Ask, Norman Geisler & Ron Brooks

Now, That's a Good Question, R.C. Sproul

Answers to Tough Questions, Reasons Skeptics Should Consider Christianity, and *Handbook of Today's Religions,* Josh McDowell & Don Stewart

Darwin on Trial, Phillip E. Johnson

My Utmost For His Highest, Oswald Chambers

Tactics, Gregory Koukl

Just as I Am, Billy Graham

Total Truth, Nancy Pearcey

How Now Shall We Live, Chuck Colson and Nancy Pearcey

The Reason for God, Tim Keller

The Historical Reliability of the New Testament, Craig Blomberg

Stealing from God, Frank Turek

Desiring God, John Piper

The Case for the Resurrection of Jesus, Habermas and Licona

The Story of Reality, Greg Koukl

Why Are There Differences in the Gospels?, Michael Licona

The Case for Christ
The Case for the Resurrection
The Case for a Creator
The Case for Faith
The Case for the Real Jesus, Lee Strobel

Foundations of Grace, Steven J. Lawson

The Emmaus Code and *Jesus on Trial*, David Limbaugh

APPS, websites, and podcasts:
Cold Case Christianity with J. Warner Wallace (J. Warner Wallace is a *Dateline* featured cold-case homicide detective, popular national speaker and best-selling author.)

Stand to Reason, str.org, Greg Koukl and other authors.

Laura Z. Powell, Blogger, laurazpowell.org

Bible Studies on various topics: mountainretreat.org

Study of Types:
http://baptistbiblebelievers.com/OTStudiesDevotionalStudiesofOldTestamentTypesWight/tabid/383/Default.aspx

https://answersingenesis.org/creation/

From the Author

This book began as my personal journey toward faith in God and His Son, Jesus Christ. It was originally meant only for the eyes of my family and friends as a testimony of my walk and why I became a Christian. I was urged by them to self–publish with the hope of reaching a wider audience.

Since then, my heart turned toward reaching the imprisoned with the Word of God. The majority of the first books printed were eventually donated to and distributed by Christian Library International (CLI), an organization whose mission is to share the Good News of Jesus Christ with the incarcerated. They will receive complimentary copies of this new edition to be forwarded to institutions throughout North America and much of the future proceeds will be donated to CLI and other Christian outreach programs. I sincerely thank you for your support.